LET GO *and* CREATE

UNLEASH CREATIVITY, BRING YOUR IDEAS TO LIFE

MARGE C. DI BLASIO

Copyright © 2020, Marge Di Blasio

All rights reserved. No part of this publication may be reproduced, distributed or transmitted in any form or by any means, including photocopying, recording, or other electronic or mechanical methods, without the prior written permission of the publisher, except in the case of brief quotations embodied in critical reviews and certain other non-commercial uses permitted by copyright law.

Although the author and publisher have made every effort to ensure that the information in this book was correct at press time, the author and publisher do not assume and hereby disclaim any liability to any party for any loss, damage, or disruption caused by errors or omissions, whether such errors or omissions result from negligence, accident, or any other cause.

Adherence to all applicable laws and regulations, including international, federal, state and local governing professional licensing, business practices, advertising, and all other aspects of doing business in the US, Canada or any other jurisdiction is the sole responsibility of the reader and consumer.

Neither the author nor the publisher assumes any responsibility or liability whatsoever on behalf of the consumer or reader of this material. Any perceived slight of any individual or organization is purely unintentional.

ISBN: 978-1-9991722-7-5 PaperBack

DOWNLOAD THE FREE RESOURCES

READ THIS FIRST
Thank you for investing in my book. As an appreciation, I'd love to give you a gift.

TO DOWNLOAD, GO TO:
https://www.margediblasio.com/letgoandcreate-freeresourcessignup

DOWNLOAD THE FREE RESOURCES

READ THIS FIRST

Thank you for investing in my book. As an appreciation, I'd love to give you a gift.

TO DOWNLOAD, GO TO:

https://www.margediblasio.com/letgoandcreate-freeresourcesignup

DEDICATION

I would like to dedicate this book to my Creator, for his unconditional love. The one who has given me the creativity and everything I value in life.

Through my writing, I found the creative flow and healing. And through my work, I hope others can be empowered and transformed us well.

CONTENTS

Preface 9

REDISCOVER YOUR CREATIVITY

Chapter 1:   What Are You Chasing After? 17
Chapter 2:   What Are You Creating? 25
Chapter 3:   Redefining Creativity 34
Chapter 4:   Fuel Your Transformation 46

LAYING A FOUNDATION FOR CREATIVITY

Chapter 5:   Let Go to Create 65
Chapter 6:   Breaking Out of Survival Mode 71
Chapter 7:   Set Goals, Not Wishes 82
Chapter 8:   Develop the Creativity within You 95

UNLOCKING YOUR CREATIVITY ROADMAP

Chapter 9:   How to Find Your Creativity 115

CREATE UNLIMITED POSSIBILITIES

Chapter 10: Making Ideas Happen 129

Conclusion 145
About The Author 151
Acknowledgments 153
Notes 155

PREFACE

Are you sitting on an idea? Like writing a book, a blog, building a business or selling a product. You want to create but can't find the perfect time.

How about the thought of creating a change in your life?

Changing careers, increasing your net worth, mending broken relationships, living a well-balanced life, or more. You're tired of doing the same thing over and over. You know that there is more to life than simply going through the motions. Inside your soul, you know that taking action towards the change will give you joy and a more fulfilling life.

Sometimes, you've taken the first few steps to get started, but as you processed all the information to do it, uncertainty kicked in and you stopped. As much as you want to change, you fear it as well. It is new, unknown, and intimidating.

Whatever you're struggling with, if you have a strong desire to bring your ideas to life but are clueless about what to do, then you've come to the right place. No matter how small or outlandish your idea can be, you can turn it into reality.

This book is about turning dreamers and consumers into Creators — people who are living intentionally, making things happen and creating significance.

Let Go and Create: Unleash Creativity, Bring Ideas to Life empowers you to break the cycle of waiting for the perfect moment, and create your best life now.

THE ORIGIN OF THIS BOOK

Like most of us, I have the desire to do many things in life. I wanted to start a business, increase my finances, expand my skill set, spend time with my family, write books, travel and more. I had an endless list of dreams to accomplish.

I started working on most of it, but the results didn't turn out how I'd expected. I read many books but never finished. I wrote stories I never published. I filled out applications and didn't hit submit. In short, I started working on my goals and then left them unfinished.

Later on, I watched my dreams unfold for others. I was thrilled to see how they created the things and life I wanted. Watching others creating gave me a taste of achieving my dreams. Then I realized, by constantly watching someone else's creation, I focused on being entertained rather than doing and ultimately sabotaged my creativity. While I am happy for those who create, deep inside, I am grieving for not turning my dreams into reality.

I asked, "Why not create?" That started me on the quest to dig deeper into creativity. It got me thinking of this phrase, '*Let Go…and Create.*'

I realized I have to let go of what stopped me from moving forward and create space for better things to enter into my life. Let go and Create! This belief got under my skin. Since then, it has become the most fundamental principle in my life.

It helped me overcome my fears, insecurities, limiting beliefs, and other unproductive habits to create the life and experience I wanted. When I moved to different countries, it allowed me to land high-paying jobs and have the courage to put myself out there despite insecurities. When I worked on my real estate license, I had six exams to pass within 18 months. I failed my test three times, but I kept trying despite being seven months pregnant, while raising my two-year-old girl, working full time, and writing my first book.

It's what fueled me to keep writing that allowed me to publish three books in less than a year. I don't say this to brag. I'm sharing this because I am certain that greater things happen when you let go of what prevents you from being at your best.

We all have a dream, but only a few dare to pursue it. When life gets busy, how will you keep your dream alive? Many times, dreams remain just daydreams for far too long.

If you are reading this book, part of you is curious about how you can create the dreams that have been chasing you for years. This is the exact reason I wrote this book for you.

Life is temporary. Situations, career jobs, people, money, opportunities come and go. We are all just passing through. That's why every second matters, create what you are called to do—the one thing that brings out the best in you and can last forever.

You have gifts, talents, and skills you are meant to share with the world. Once you embrace the power of creativity, you will be amazed by what you can accomplish. You can start where you are, with what you have, and create what you wish existed.

After studying, researching, interviewing other creators, I have learned valuable and hard lessons along the way. Everything that I discovered, that transformed my life and the lives of many dramatically–you are about to gain in this book. As you go through each page, follow the steps provided, and learn from other creators. You can bring your ideas to life. You can create your best life now.

HOW THIS BOOK WILL BENEFIT YOU

Let Go and Create will encourage, inspire, and transform your life. You can use it for creating your first book, blog, or start simple projects. You can apply it to start your business, build a company, create financial freedom, a healthy lifestyle, or even relationships. Most of all, you can use this to turn your ideas into reality and spread creativity in your life, family, organization, community, and create a significant change.

In the pages that follow, I will share a detailed plan for creating better habits that will guide you to achieve your goal. It consists of ten chapters that will show you where you are in your creative walk and the massive opportunities available to you. It includes empowering stories of ordinary people like you and me who dream once, and now create what they wish existed.

To start with, I have to set your expectations. There is no one right way to create your best life or whatever you want, but this book describes the best way I know—an approach that will be effective regardless of where you start or what you're trying to change. The strategies I cover will be relevant to anyone looking for a step-by-step system for improvement, whether your goals center on health, money, productivity, relationships, or all of the above. As long as you want to make space to create, this book will be your guide.

LET GO AND CREATE

No matter what your circumstances are, you can break the cycle of waiting for the perfect moment, and start to create your best life now.

1
WHAT ARE YOU CHASING AFTER?

> *When you stop chasing the wrong*
> *things, you give the right things*
> *a chance to catch you.*
> *- Lolly Daskal*

From an early age, we are taught that more is better. More money, time, things, security, work, relationships, power or sometimes, just consuming more. We are living in a society that encourages us that the more we possess in life, the better position we are in.

We get so busy chasing all the things we haven't got, that we take for granted the things we already have. The people in our lives, the fortunate circumstances we are in, the gift of creativity and unique abilities born with us.

We keep chasing for more in pursuit of temporary happiness, then fail to realize that there is a better way.

The result is, we lose touch with our creative side. We restrict ourselves to a small zone of comfort and miss out on most of the best things. We make decisions that cause us to suffer more from our losses than what we gained in life.

What are you chasing after?

Are you chasing after temporary pleasures or lifelong joy?

Whatever you are pursuing, defines what you are creating at the moment.

In my case, it was all about my career. I grew up believing that getting a job was the best way to earn money. I knew money wasn't everything, but if you came from a place of survival, it plays a more significant role in happiness and health than you may think.

In many third world countries, poverty limits your access to almost everything: food, shelter, education and healthcare. People mourned for dying family or friends because they couldn't afford to get medical treatment. It causes stress and depression that could lead to violent crime.

Growing up in this environment motivated me at a young age to make more money. I wanted to help others and never be in that situation again. At the same time, I felt the pressure to make good out of everything I do. As I climbed the ladder to achieve my goal, I didn't realize I had lost touch with my creativity – the engineer of a fulfilled life.

IN PURSUIT OF MORE

I've loved the arts ever since I was a little kid. It started when I fell in love with two paintings hung on the white wall in my living room. Oil paintings of a sunset sailboat seascape and horses racing. The level of work and creativity invested by the artists in their creations fascinated my young imagination. The harmonious matching of colors, shorter brushstrokes, symbolic images, and sketches captivated my soul.

I stared at those artworks constantly and I couldn't get them out of my head. It inspired me to create. I drew the same image every day for a few months. Even my brothers mocked and insulted my work; I kept drawing. The first few weeks were hard but each day, the results got a little better.

After three months, I created duplicate sketches of the artwork that I was finally proud of. When I ultimately shared the result with others, the mocking and insults turned to praise and encouragement.

In times I didn't paint or draw, I wrote poems, letters and stories. I played in my imaginary world with different characters and places. I read books that allowed me to see a bigger world, to travel to different places and to meet different people.

These were magical times when I felt so alive. All of a sudden I had to go to university and everything changed.

I thought of taking Fine Arts, but the question of how I would make a living discouraged me. If I couldn't choose a subject related to my passion, what would I do?

Like many young people, I observed and listened to others' opinions. Everyone said that IT could lead to a high-paying job, so I went in that direction. The path I thought to a better life.

After a few years, I established a successful career. I focused on improving my skills and building relationships. I worked my way up to get better options. Promotions, work flexibility, travel, salary increase, bonuses, cool gadgets, and exposure to different technology. Innovation surrounded me. It was an exciting journey.

My accomplishments helped me survive and even thrive until I realized, part me of wasn't growing as it should. As I reached my goals, I recognized that the direction I headed wasn't where I dreamt of being.

I was grateful to have a job but deep inside, I felt like I was dying. Even though I was a top performer, worked with some fantastic people and earned more, something was missing. I knew I gave my best, but recognized that my achievements didn't mean fulfillment. As Tony Robbins says, "Success without fulfillment is the ultimate failure." And that's exactly how I felt.

Have you ever been in a situation when you felt something was wrong?

When you said to yourself, "there is more to life than this"?

Don't get me wrong; I didn't drop everything or quit my job after that realization. I'm also not encouraging you to make an extreme decision when you face a similar situation. But if you encounter these thoughts, I'm asking you to pay attention to them, because there are reasons why they came to you.

Thoughts serve as clues of what we search for in our lives. Understanding your thoughts will help you reach your full potential. So please, for your benefit, don't shut them down. Use them as an opportunity to assess your life.

If you face the same situation, here are some questions to guide you in making decisions:

- Is what I do still aligned with my values and priorities?
- Is what I do align with my life's purpose?
- Is trading my time for what I do, with what matters most to me, worth it?
- Are there other ways to do it?
- Am I giving my best?

LET GO AND CREATE

- Is there another place I want to be? Are there other things I want to do rather than this?
- What's stopping me from doing what I want?

As you ponder the questions above, you will have a good start assessing where you are in life. These questions clarified where I was and directed me to create what I truly wanted.

Stop chasing what your mind wants, and you'll get what your soul needs.

ACTION CHALLENGE

What did you today that cheered your soul?

Even if you spent a little time on it and haven't seen the result yet; you are still proud of yourself for taking action.

If you can think of one thing, that's good. You are in a much better position than many people around you. I encourage you to reflect on what you have created and the next step you'll take.

If you can't think of anything yet, don't worry. It's not too late to start. Get moving and start creating.

INSPIRATIONAL REFLECTION

To help you along the way, I've included a "dose of inspirational stories" in some sections of this book. These are real stories of ordinary people, just like you and me, who committed to take action to turn their ideas into reality. Despite all the fears of stepping into the unknown, they took a leap, and that decision transformed their lives.

As you read the stories, I encourage you to allow yourself to be infused entirely with the motivation to take action. If others do it, you can do it too. Believe that this is one of your first steps to take action towards your creativity!

FROM SHY KID TO SOCIAL MEDIA INFLUENCER

Nuseir Yassin grew up in Arraba, a small agricultural city in northern Israel. He came from a modest middle-class family.

A middle child of four; his parents, who worked as teacher and psychologist, valued education and hard work. Growing up, he was shy and socially awkward.

Hungry for an education at a prestigious university, he got a scholarship from Harvard and graduated with a degree in Economics. After that, he moved to New York City to work.

He started working as a software developer for Venmo, a mobile payment service owned by PayPal and earned over $100,000 per year.

Despite having a high-paying job, he realized something was missing. He wasn't fulfilled and was tired of his daily routine. So, he spent a year and a half saving up $60,000. In 2016, he quit his job, bought a camera, a plane ticket, and traveled around the world.

He adopted the moniker "Nas"– Arabic for "people"– and set up a Facebook page called Nas Daily, where he committed to documenting every day of his travels. He pledged to make a single video every day for 1,000 days.

In one of his interviews, he said, "I don't usually take risks, but I decided to make use of every single day. I didn't want to waste a single minute."

His first destination, Kenya, proved to be a fruitful one. A Russia-owned media company operating out of Nairobi saw one of his early videos and offered to pay him to create content for their Facebook pages. The company paid him $3,000 a month for his services. It allowed him to continue traveling comfortably and granted him the exposure he needed to build an audience.

> *We have busy lives. But everyone has a spare minute.*
> *- Nas Daily.*

His creation has inspired many people to travel and learn more about different cultures. He finished the 1000 daily video journey on January 5, 2019. Now, Nas has a video making company and approximately 14M followers on social media.

Like most of us, Nas wasn't comfortable taking the risk when he started. But his desire to not waste a single minute and to make the most of every single day was stronger than being uncomfortable. Like what Nas did, you too can create that change you want and find the path to a fulfilling life.

2

WHAT ARE YOU CREATING?

*Your life is your art. What
are you creating today?*
— author unknown

Think of the people you admire because of the "wow" factor that they bring into this world. Wherever you are, whatever you're doing, stop for a minute and ask yourself what makes you follow these individuals. Is it their inventions, breath-taking creations, luxurious lifestyle, witty sense of humor, authentic life, or significant mark in this world?

Here's who I think about: Elon Musk, Oprah Winfrey, Marie Forleo, Bill Gates, John Maxwell. Aside from being founders of large companies that created jobs for many, they are also known as change-makers. They see the world differently than most, continually trying new things, stretching themselves and making a difference in the lives of others.

There's a good chance that you and I follow people because of what they create. Whatever they do, inspires, transforms, entertains or influences you. What makes them create? Were they born creative and gifted with all the skills needed to succeed?

The truth is, the creators you admire are ordinary people like you and me. We all have 24 hours a day and many commitments in life. Whatever they created started with an idea, a thought, then they took action. Most of them are clueless about what to do next and are not comfortable taking a risk. Despite all the hesitation, they take the first step.

Do you realize that almost everything we have now was once thought?

Look around you. Each building that surrounds you, every device you use, every movie you've seen, the books you've read, the songs you've listened to, the vehicles you used to travel to different places, all started from a single thought to become reality. As Marie Forloe said, "Everything in the material world is first created on the level of thought."

The thing is, many of us are an audience of other's creations. Following others gives us a taste of their world. It allows us to experience the dreams we wish we could have. What we need to watch out for is when we become full-time followers and stop creating.

PEOPLE WHO CREATE, FOCUS ON EXECUTION.

Inspiration and motivation make you feel good, but it is the action you will do next that will make a difference. Even if that action leads to failure, get up again, learn from it and move on. Fail forward.

WHAT REALITY ARE YOU CREATING FOR YOURSELF?

*If you don't make the time to work on
creating the life you want, you're eventually*

going to be forced to spend a LOT of time dealing with a life you don't want.
- Kevin Ngo, Let's Do This!

I used to be a full-time audience for other's creativity. I turned on the television, looked at social media and followed other's creations. I watched my dreams unfold vicariously. I was thrilled to see how many people got their books published, spoke at conferences, traveled to different places, invested in different things and spent more time with whoever they wanted. I thought they won the lottery to have all the time and resources.

Then I realized it's not luck. Creators make things happen. By constantly watching someone else's creation, I focused on being entertained rather than doing. It got me thinking, "If I'm not creating the life I want now, then what am I making?"

I realized I was not creating what I wanted. I was waiting for the perfect time, as defined by the standard of society: when the kids are older, when I have enough money, when I can retire or when the right time comes.

I thought the things that kept me busy would fulfill my goals and make the life of my dreams. Instead, the negative feelings got on my nerves. Stress and anxiety got a hold of me. My life choices impacted my priorities before I even recognized it. Inside my soul, I knew something must change. And the only way to change it, was to stop escaping and to deal with my reality.

To create what I love now, I had to go back to the places where I could unleash my creativity. To revisit the moments that reminded me to create something. To allow myself to embrace the process of creation, and this is what I'm recommending you to do.

Knowing what you want to create is good, but it won't lead you in the right direction. Not until you start taking action.

In my case, I decided to take small steps every day to create. Despite many commitments, sleepless nights with my little kids, a stressful job and more, I worked towards my goals. My conviction to turn my dreams into reality was so strong that I chose creation versus consumption.

After a few months, I progressed in my goals but not in the direction I wanted. As much as I wanted to change, I wrestled with my fears as well. I asked myself, "Can I really do this? What if it doesn't work out? What will others think?"

The fear was intimidating. Then one day, I received a call. My mother-in-law had died. My heart crashed to the floor. I was devastated.

She was one of the most brilliant, caring, and giving people I've ever met. She encouraged me to pursue learning, to continue growing without compromising my priorities. She taught me how to aim high and not be afraid to be true to myself. Months after that, I learned that other friends had died as well and the news was filled with death every day. I couldn't stop thinking about it all.

No matter how prepared you think you are for the death of a loved one, it still comes as a shock and is heartbreaking. We reminisce about how talented, loving, caring they were and how fortunate we were to know them. We remind ourselves that we wouldn't trade those moments for the world. Then we ponder how much more they could have brought into this world, but they are gone.

As heartbreak crashed over me, I realized that today is all I have because tomorrow is not guaranteed.

"Knowing that you have limited time, what are you creating?"

As I pondered these thoughts, my focus shifted. My fear of being uncomfortable transformed to the fear of not living life to the fullest. I grieved, then decided to take action to make each day my masterpiece.

Be true to yourself, help others, make each day your masterpiece, make friendship a fine art, drink deeply from good books - especially the Bible, build a shelter against a rainy day, give thanks for your blessings and pray for guidance every day.
John Wooden

As a result of those actions, I've gone from being a dreamer to a doer. I transformed from someone who hardly accomplished goals to a finisher. I achieved my creative goals sooner than I planned. I published books, created an online course, developed a healthier lifestyle, wrote content that changed people's lives and spent more quality time with the people that matter to me.

I reconnected with my creativity and transformed what I chased after into something bigger. It's no longer about money or having a self-centered better life. It's about creating a life with intention, significance, and fullness. I found the joy I've been longing for and fulfillment in life.

What about you? If today is your last day, would you be facing it without regrets? Have you given your best to create what you are supposed to do?

You may have a strong desire to create your dreams, but you don't know how to proceed. You know there is more inside of you. But something has to change for you to create your dreams and to rise to your fullest. You're holding on to what you have now, your precious life.

Let go of the non-essential things. You don't need your entire day to start creating. Begin where you are, use what you have. Start with a little time, thirty minutes or an hour creating the desires of your heart if you want to experience having creativity back in your life. It's a matter of how hungry you are to create your best life now.

Are you willing to create the best that life has to offer you?

EVERY SECOND IS A GIFT TO CREATE THE LIFE YOU WANT. BUILD THE THINGS YOU WISH EXISTED.

ACTION CHALLENGE:

"...There is more to life than pleasing people. There is much more to life than following others' prescribed path. There is so much more to life than what you experience right now. You need to decide who you are for yourself. Become a whole being. Adventure."
—Roy T. Bennett

If you don't know where you are, you can't get where you're going. Grab a journal. Take some time to reflect on the questions below and write it down. Remember, you won't get results by keeping all your answers in your head.

What are the things that kept me busy?

What's the ultimate return I can get out of what I do now?

Does my answer to these questions make me feel fulfilled? If not, what can I change now to get a better result?

INSPIRATIONAL REFLECTION

IT'S NEVER TOO LATE TO CREATE!

Do you think it's too late for you to create what you want?

Today, the most popular images of creators, entrepreneurs, innovators are young people. However, some famous people became successful in their creation later in life. With time, they gained the wisdom and clarity that allowed them to build their empires strategically.

One of the most prominent creative individuals in the fashion world is Vera Wang. She is one of the most celebrated bridal wear designers. But did you know that she did not even begin designing clothes professionally until her 40s?

Vera was born and raised in New York City and is of Chinese descent. From the age of six, she started figure skating. In high school, she competed in the United States Figure Skating Championship.

After years of intensive competition, she didn't make it to the 1968 US Olympics team. Her initial dream of a career as an Olympic figure skater didn't take off. It was then that she diverted her attention to the fashion industry.

Upon her graduation from college, she began working as a fashion editor with Vogue. She got promoted to senior fashion editor and stayed in this role for 17 years. She later worked as a design director for Ralph Lauren for two years.

When she was planning her wedding, at 40, she found herself confounded by the lack of bridal gowns for older and more mature brides. Everywhere she went, the dresses were overdone with too many frills and lace. She couldn't find anything simple, elegant, or even remotely sexy.

She ended up hiring a dressmaker to create a custom-made gown, which ended up costing $10,000. Her bridal adventures got her thinking that other women could face similar problems in finding the right dress. This experience led her to create her bridal salon, selling dresses from top designers around the world. Her wedding gown boutiques have been opened in Australia, Sydney, Tokyo, London and New York. Today she's one of the world's premier women's designers.

> *"When you fall down — which you have to [do] if you want to learn to be a skater — you pick yourself right up and start again. You don't let anything deter you. Oddly enough, it's strangely like fashion — you have a limited amount of time in which to get a point of view across."*
> *– Vera Wang*

Good things take time. They don't happen overnight. Often you will have to go through many experiences in life. Sometimes, it is not the best place where you want to be, but you have to go through it. Because it is where you develop your character.

When the right time comes, when the opportunity arises, you're ready to create your big one. Don't worry about how late you start. What matters is to have the courage to make it happen.

REDEFINING CREATIVITY

The best artists, scientists, engineers, inventors, entrepreneurs, and other creators are the ones who keep taking steps by finding new problems, new solutions, and then new problems again.
- Kevin Ashton

What is Creativity?

The English word *creativity* comes from the Latin term *creare*. *Creare* means to create or make.

Webster's dictionary defined it as the ability or power to create, to bring into existence, to invest with a new form or to produce through imaginative skill.

Rollo May, the author of <u>The Courage to Create</u> said, "Creativity is the process of bringing something new into being. It requires passion and commitment. It brings to our awareness what was previously hidden and points to new life."

Creativity means many things to different people. We typically associate it with arts, music, dance, theatre, but it is how you live your life each day, what you do and why you do it. With all your energy, thoughts, words and actions, you are creating your life.

As human beings, we are born to create. Where do you spend your time? How do you live your life?

Here is my illustration of how creativity can be defined:

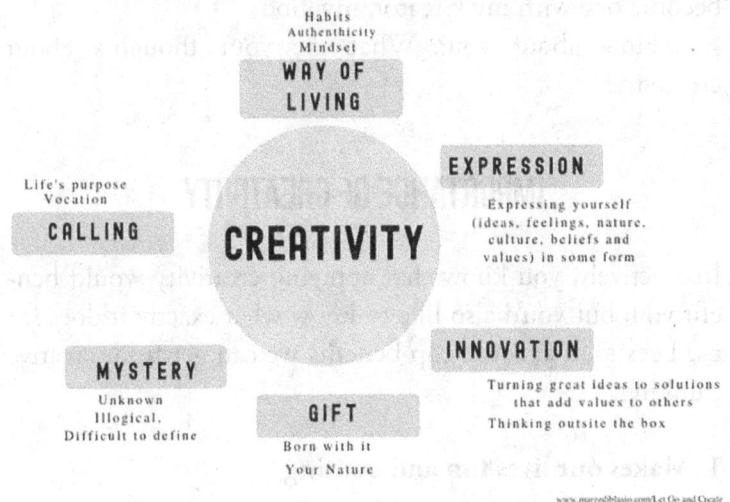

Creativity is an *expression or feeling* you get when you experience something better than ordinary. Many define it as a gift; you are born with it. It is human nature.

Others define creativity as a *way of living*. Even though you are born with it, you need to continue to nurture and cultivate it as part of your daily life.

Alternatively, people believe it is a *vocation or calling*, your life's purpose. Nobody can take it away from you.

You could even say *creativity and innovation go hand in hand*. It is when great ideas are turned into solutions that value is added to many. To others, creativity remains a mystery.

For me, when I learned to let go of all my limiting beliefs, it made the space to create. As I embraced the process of creativity, I discovered more about my Creator, myself, others, and my purpose.

Creativity makes me feel alive. When I fully immersed myself in the process of creation and tapped into my source I become one with my Creator, my God.

How about you? What are your thoughts about creativity?

IMPORTANCE OF CREATIVITY

Instinctively, you know that applying creativity would benefit you, but you'd also like to know what exactly it does for us. Let's look at seven top benefits we can get from creative thinking:

1. Makes our lives fun and exciting

Many people pursue a creative hobby or outlet because it makes them feel good. It's something to look forward to outside your routine. It makes you jump out of bed and look forward to the new day.

It gives you hope that every day is another opportunity to live with creativity – the life that embraces originality and imagination with wide-open arms.

It's something you can turn to if you've had a bad day. Knowing you have a creative medium that's yours, contributes to building a positive self-identity.

2. Predicts a longer life

Nicholas Turiano stated in a Scientific American article that, "Researchers found that only creativity, not intelligence or overall openness—decreased mortality risk. One possible reason creativity is protective of health is because it draws on a variety of neural networks within the brain. Individuals high in creativity maintain the integrity of their neural networks even into old age." A notion supported by a January study from Yale University that correlated openness with the robustness of study subjects' white matter, which promotes connections between neurons in different parts of the brain. Because the brain is the command center for all bodily functions, exercising it helps all systems to continue running smoothly.

He also cites, "Keeping the brain healthy may be one of the most important aspects of aging successfully—a fact shown by creative persons living longer in our study."

James Clear, the author of Atomic Habits, also cites studies and research that demonstrates creating art decreases negative emotions, reduces stress and anxiety, and improves medical outcomes. Not only can being creative help you live longer, but it can improve your quality of health and life too.

3. Solve problems

Being creative helps you become a better problem solver in all areas of your life. Instead of coming from a linear or logical approach, your creative side can approach a situation from all angles. Creativity helps you see things differently and deal with uncertainty better. Studies show that creative people are better able to live with uncertainty because they can adapt their thinking to allow for the flow of the unknown.

Although creativity also comes with many ups and downs and a high risk of failure, it helps you develop your confidence every time you create.

4. Connects you with your Higher Self - remembering your nature

Stoking the fires of creativity is helping you remember who you are and your gifts. Being creative gives you opportunities to try out new ideas and explore different ways of thinking and problem-solving.

You don't need to dream up anything big; in fact, starting small may be the wisest choice. Each word spoken, phrase sang, brush stroke, letter typed, dance steps taken, will access more of your spirit and your creative nature. Each will lead you on a path to the unexpected where aliveness waits for you.

5. Form of Medication - it's Therapeutic

Researchers found that creativity affects the brain and body, leading to benefits like increased mood, decreased anxiety, heightened cognitive function, reduced risk of chronic illnesses and improved immune health.

John Silva, a film producer, mentioned in his interview that he created his cinematic three-minute videos as he finds it therapeutic for himself.

Elizabeth Gilbert, the author of Big Magic, said that she continues to write, despite rejections and results in her early career in writing, because she loves it.

6. Creativity is a competitive tool

It's a fundamental human reality; you need to succeed no matter how you live. Whether you're an entrepreneur, work for a large company, or a solo creative person, it's what makes you stand out.

In 2010 studies conducted by IBM, a survey of 1,500 Chief Executive Officers from 60 countries and 33 industries worldwide, chief executives believe that successfully navigating an increasingly complex world would require creativity. More than rigor, management discipline, integrity, or even vision—it's the way you can distinguish yourself and the way you can innovate.

7. Makes the world a better place

You have a unique creative gift that only YOU can unleash. As you do, you'll be surprised at your capacity to create great work. As a result, there will be more people that will be inspired, encouraged, entertained, or transformed.

What seems simple to you is often brilliant to someone else. But you'll never know that unless you learn to let go of what's in your hands and tap into your creativity.

The creative process invites everyone to be creative. The world needs people who put creative work out into the world.

ACTION CHALLENGE:

Start journaling, write a poem or jot down what you feel or think. Doodle, draw your next picture without judgment or fear and see what happens. Keep it simple and fun.

Don't worry about doing it wrong. Don't wait until you know it all or have it all. Just ease in and take advantage of everything creativity has to offer.

INSPIRATIONAL REFLECTIONS

FROM OBSERVER TO CREATOR

In 2010 I moved to Canada from Singapore, got married and started a new job. All the changes to my environment, culture, weather, family and workplace happened all at once. I didn't realize how badly it impacted my health and life until I could no longer manage the anxiety and stress it caused. I sought professional help and this is where I met someone special, let's call her Yang.

From the first time I met Yang, her positive aura in life captivated me. She helped me, and many people to find their voices, strengths, and selves again.

Yang helped me realize that rising to my full potential could be challenging. She provided me the support I needed on my journey. What amazed me more is that she remained a humble and kind-hearted individual despite her achievements, expertise, and business success. She empowers many people and her work reflects her values in life. She believes in creating what everyone wishes existed.

When I started working on this book, I asked her how she created her business and her thoughts about Creativity. Here's her story:

"My entrepreneurial mindset started early, as many of my relatives are farmers. Since I was ten, we had a small vegetable business. When I was 17, my older sister bought a vegetable market business. I bought it from her and ran it for four years.

Each time I have owned a business, I felt like it wasn't even of my own doing or choosing, it just happened and I leaned into it. If you want something, create it. Don't depend or rely on anyone for anything. So, it is in my fiber to create and be a leader of my own life.

For years, I worked in different places where I learned about different ways, styles and approaches to business. It gave me valuable information for creating the experience I wanted for myself, clients and other people to work with. I quickly decided to leave and put a plan together when I realized it was no longer a fit.

Contrast gave clarity. Sometimes, it's important to know what you want, but I have found it can be just as important to know what you don't want.

I got to the point of clarity. Once I had the vision, I created an action plan, then I moved from there."

THOUGHTS ABOUT CREATIVITY

"To create is being open and surrendering to Life, God, or whatever you believe in. It connects you to creativity, to see what the day will bring, who you can help and what to say or do. All things that exist are born out of creative thought. A thought comes and ignites people/organizations to do/be, something. It can transform something into something even more.

The thing is, we can all create - whether that be our relationships, our work, hobbies, mood or well-being. It's endless. It's a mental state to be open and receptive to create. It is a state of surrender as sometimes the creation differs from what you thought it should be."

IN APPLYING CREATIVITY

"When I create, I picture tapping into the source of life - to motivate and fill me with inspiration.

I created various businesses and a family. I renovated my home and learned to build furniture. I do woodworking, sewing, cooking and baking and more because I wanted those experiences. I find time to create what I want.

If you want to nurture your creativity, just do it. Put yourself into something for the sheer sake of it.

In my case, I started painting and just explored it. I have never thought of myself as creative artistically, but I ended up loving it. Were the paintings beautiful? Not really, but I enjoyed doing it.

I think what it brings to me is more important than the result. I find it pleasing and therapeutic. I even gave them away, which was difficult because of judgment. Then I saw one of my paintings at a thrift store a few months later. It was hard!

Then I realized, what matters most is that I stepped into my creativity. It took courage to share my work with others despite the possibilities of rejection and criticism.

As Mother Teresa's said, "it is between you and God; it was never between you and them." I believe that life is working for me and continue to create the things I wish existed."

VULNERABILITY IN CREATIVITY

"When I started my business, it was a way out of my comfort zone. I was stepping into the unknown. I had to deal with contracts, leases and accounting. I did not enjoy all the logistical stuff. It made me very anxious and nervous, but it was a stepping stone to reach my goal.

Being self-employed is such a vulnerable experience -financially, emotionally and mentally. I consider it to be a spiritual experience, which for me, I'm honored to have through my work.

The rewarding part is knowing that I could do more than I thought. I realized that it is possible to create a successful business or anything you want with integrity.

Also, people seem to love to judge and make comments about those who try to put themselves out there. It's vulnerable and often met with discussions or comments. I found this challenging, but now see it for what it is. People judge, it is our human nature. It will always be a part of anyone's life who is choosing to be authentic and vulnerable."

IN DEALING WITH CHALLENGES

"During tough times, I prayed and focused on my vision. Knowing that what I do and why I do it is for me, for my distinct relationship with life. It doesn't need to make sense to others. I also have two incredible friends that remind me of who I am when I forget or feel afraid."

WORDS OF WISDOM

"My grandpa, who loved woodworking, told me it's better to do many things at 90% than only a few at 100%. I lived by it. I work hard and do my best, but I don't need perfection to be a part of everything. I also like the SFD concept - "shitty first draft."

Get to the writing or doing whatever you are working on and not to worry about the final draft at the very beginning. Get moving, don't stagnate with details. Creativity needs movement."

—m—

For Yang, becoming an entrepreneur is not even a path she could imagine to pursue. As she listened to her inner voice, surroundings and life, she ended up creating the business that led her to create the life she wanted.

Our beliefs determine whether we fail or succeed, and how we define success in the first place. Yang identified where her beliefs came from and took the steps needed.

How about you? Are you ready to face the greater things that life can offer once you step into your creativity?

FUEL YOUR TRANSFORMATION

Creativity is contagious. Pass it on.
- *Albert Einstein*

When you create, you discover more about yourself. This discovery leads to clarity, about who you are, what you want, why you exist and how to proceed with the next steps. As you allow yourself to let go and embrace the process of creation, you will enter the creative flow.

Creative flow is the state where you are present and fully immersed in creation. Your mind is fully open and attuned to the act of creating. You become one with your Creator and the universe.

Csikszentmihalyi explained the state of 'creative flow' very well in his February 2004 TED talk.

He said, "There's this focus that, once it becomes intense, leads to a sense of ecstasy, a sense of clarity: you know exactly what you want to do from one moment to the other; you get immediate feedback. You know that what you need to do is possible to do, even though difficult, and the sense of time disappears, you forget yourself, you feel part of something larger. And once *the conditions are present, what you are doing becomes worth doing for its own sake."*

What a powerful truth - when you are in creative flow, outside distraction recedes from your consciousness and there are no boundaries.

If you think you're not creative, unmotivated, unsure of yourself and clueless how to change your situation - you're not alone. Most people are in the same boat, but you can take action now to get out of that rut.

Find out what it takes and see what you've got. Life gives you clues. When you take action towards creating, you will eventually experience the creative flow. Tap into creativity to reveal your hidden talents and gifts. If you never explore, you will never know.

TRANSFORMATION IN CREATIVITY

I encourage you to take action now to bring your dreams and ideas to life. From the moment you start, it will have a positive, lasting effect on you.

If you're still not ready to take that first step, here's more on how Creativity will transform you:

1. Bring out the Best in You

In life, it's not what we get that makes us valuable; it is what we become in the process that brings value to our lives. When you assume responsibility in your life to create, you will find your voice, develop your character and you will experience inner fulfillment.

When you create, you will gain the confidence to speak and live out what you believe in front of others. When you face challenges, you will grow and develop because you see struggles as opportunities to bring out the best in you.

When you take action towards creativity, you'll find contentment. You will realize it is where you are supposed to be. It is when your actions become aligned with who you are.

This is what my long-time friend, Mae Flores, experienced when she learned to let go of the things she was holding on to. She chose to be in partnership with her Creator and stepped into creativity. That changed the direction of her life.

FINDING YOUR CREATIVE PURPOSE

I met Mae a long time ago in Singapore. She had a stable job, but she felt she had to go back to her homeland in the Philippines.

She worked in various departments, from Sales to Operations, and was a Project Manager for years. The last time we talked, things had transformed in her life.

I told her I was working on my third book and asked her thoughts about creativity. To my surprise, she said that she creates every day, and that's what brings alignment to her priorities in life.

She said, "One thing that kills creativity is routine. It's important not to follow structures at all times. It's good to get lost sometimes because you discover unlimited possibilities. It helps to unleash your creativity, find innovative ideas, and gain new experience that will lead you to a more fulfilled life."

Mae shared her story of how her choices helped her to find her voice, develop her character and allowed her to experience inner fulfillment.

"I quit my job as a Project Manager. I followed what God called me to do. I accepted a full-time position in the church even though others didn't understand my decision. I wasn't sure if everything would go well. I was worried about the unknown, but deep inside, I knew I had to obey.

Despite fear and doubts, I followed my heart. Since then, I found the peace I longed for. I never looked back. I quit my excellent job, and it turned out to be the catalyst for something greater. It was the best decision I have ever made.

I wear many hats in my position, but I don't mind it. I work as a Corporate Secretary, National Coordinator, Administrative Manager, Church Leader, Children Ministry Teacher and many other roles. When there is a need, I'm willing to step in.

One of the things I'm doing now is serving the kids in the Children Ministry. Many of them are from the Bangkal, Makati neighborhood in Manila. It is a typical small and close-knit community in Makati, outside the central business district and high-end areas.

In this ministry, we have classes and activities organized for children every week. They come to a place that allows them to connect with others, to learn, be inspired and entertained.

Some kids come from low-income families and struggle each day to meet their basic needs. Coming to an environment where they feel safe is beneficial for them. They feel loved and supported.

As a staff member, I have to plan for this. We need to have committed teachers to equip the kids. If you want to create a life with significance, you need to commit to contributing. You need to be a lifelong learner, a teacher, while always listening to the desires of your heart. This makes finding resources challenging at certain times.

When we started, we lacked experience. We were not equipped, but through faith and prayer, we made it happen. Together with the team, I learned to trust God to give us wisdom. He gave us guidance and direction. We built our faith in him and in ourselves. It was a partnership. We leaned into our Creator and as his co-creator, we took actions.

Mae Flores together with the kids in Children Ministry

Eventually, we saw how he transformed each of us in this ministry and the lives of the children. The transformation continued to flow to their families. It's rewarding to make that significant contribution together with God and my team.

As a team, we grew and learned to work together. We now focus more on solutions and empower creative work instead of fixating on the problems.

We encountered many challenges along the road. As a leader, I'm constantly learning how to be more effective in my approach. I developed strategies for guiding others and leading them to God. During difficult times, I pray to God, my Creator, and surrender all my burdens into His loving hands. He gives me peace, wisdom and direction.

I'm also pursuing a Master's Degree in Social Development with a Specialization in Policy Research and Practice. I want to serve these kids more effectively. They are the reason I'm doing this; they are my inspiration.

The rewarding part of my journey is to make significant contributions to the lives of these kids now, even before I finish my master's degree."

It has truly been a pleasure working with God and to create something new and original in this world. We experience good and bad things, but it makes us grow. Know that God can work in you and is at work in you. Put your confidence in God instead of yourself.
- Mae Flores

A few years ago, Mae never saw herself working in the church, going to graduate school or serving kids with different needs. By allowing herself to step into the unknown, she is living her life to the fullest.

She doesn't work just for money anymore. She is doing what she is called to do, living a life with purpose and creating significance in the lives of others.

Remember, when your actions are aligned with who you are, you find contentment, inner fulfillment, and are no longer afraid to use your voice.

If you want to experience the fullness of life, let go of the things you're holding onto and create on the right path.

2. Connects You to Others

As you tap into your creativity, you will connect with other creative individuals. People who inspire and motivate you to take a leap, build your dreams and create the life you want.

I experienced this when I worked on my first book, <u>One Step At A Time: How To Turn Your Adversities To Opportunities</u>. I had no idea what to do when I started writing. I only knew the reasons why I did it. I wanted to share my story. I knew that if one person would be inspired and transformed with my book, it would be worth it. And lastly, I was creating my legacy.

I had a strong desire to create it, so I searched for free materials online on how to write a book. I started writing and followed the steps I learned, but I wanted to get it done sooner. I knew that surrounding myself with people who published books and were on the same writing journey would be the most effective way.

I enrolled in a self-publishing course and joined a community where I got to know like-minded people—aspiring authors who believed in their message and wanted to share it with the world.

Surrounding myself with the right people helped me to have the right mindset, skills, and resources I needed. After decades of wishing to share my story, I published my book in four months. This is also where I met Anita Oomen.

CREATIVITY CHAIN

Anita Oommen is a Speech-Language Pathologist and Audiologist. She has worked for a United Nations Development Program, helping under-resourced and under-privileged children with disabilities.

She is also the best-selling author of Picking Up The Shards: Healing the Pain of Mother-Wounds, Discovering the Mother-Heart of God. In her book, she shared her gut-wrenching personal account of childhood trauma, neglect, rejection and abuse.

I had the privilege to support Anita in her book launch. Although our lives are unique, our stories resonate. We have the same mission of sharing the message of hope to those in need. To spread the news that dark moments in life don't determine our destiny. To continue to step out of our comfort zone, lean on our Creator, and to strive for our best to live to the fullest.

Another thing we have in common is that we both have two young kids. What inspired me more about Anita is when I found out that her kids had already published their books.

Her daughter Alaina, is the author of The Very Friendly Poodle, which she published when she was eleven, and her youngest son Ian, is the author of This is How Ian Rolls at the age of seven.

It's always been my desire to co-author a book with my daughters, but I couldn't imagine when it would be the right time until I saw what Anita's kids had done.

I told Anita that my daughter was impacted when she read her son's book, but we may need to wait when she is a little older. To my surprise, Anita encouraged me more when she said, "My son created this story at four. When he is in kindergarten."

Anita's story motivated me to serve as inspiration to my kids and to support them to nurture their creativity. I dropped my belief that what an individual can create is limited by his or her age.

Creativity has no limits. Allow yourself to go through the process and let the creativity flow.

That's what I did with my oldest daughter Arwen. When I asked her if she wanted us to create her book, she said 'yes' with a huge smile.

I grabbed my pen and paper and started writing it down as Arwen narrated her story. Then I read it back to her, asked her thoughts on the characters, and how she wanted the illustrations. The look on her face showed excitement and curiosity.

I passed the blank sheets of paper, and she started working on her drawings. At her young age, she created the first draft of her book and was eager to proceed with the next steps. Her creative ideas were unlimited.

It was one of my defining moments. I realized Arwen needed support and encouragement on my end to nurture more of her creativity. As a parent, we play an essential role to cultivate the creativity of our kids.

As individuals, I believe we have the same purpose. The world can be a much better place if we have more creative people. The creative process invites everyone to change the world.

From connecting with other like-minded people like Anita, to collaborating with my four-year-old child, I learned a lesson about the limitless creativity we can cultivate with one another. We just need to let go of our limiting beliefs.

That is what Creativity does. While in the process of executing an idea, you will encounter a chain reaction of many tiny sparks. It connects you to others and continues to expand around you. It's unstoppable. As you tap in, you see bigger opportunities to create and encourage others to create.

3. Multiply Your Creativity

Once you create, it will continue to show you limitless opportunities to create more. This is what happened when I met Asmaa Doomak.

I've never met Asmaa in person, but she supported me in my book launch.

She said, "It's my first time to read a book that touched my heart like that. In each part, I felt a good feeling, something inspirational, and full of positivity that makes you keep reading. Congratulations, I knew it would be a best seller. I even shared it with my friends…"

It cheered my soul. I created the book because I wanted to. Knowing others get empowered with what I created, motivates me to do more.

This is how creativity works. Creating nurtures creativity. It allowed me to create more books, courses, and to live a life by design, not by default.

Both Asmaa and I have the same goal of using the platform of writing to create a life of significance. She is the author of You are Unique: Live Your Life As It Suits You. She wrote a book to help girls and women in Egypt and the Arab world to love themselves and raise their self-confidence.

Recently, Asmaa created a campaign for empowerment for teenage girls and young adults. In this campaign, Asma shared her story.

"Working on my master project was a chance to know about the Geographic Information Systems (GIS) field by coincidence. I like that it has applications in almost every field.

During my masters, I read more about it and attended lectures with younger students. I did it till I got a job as a teaching assistant. Since then, I started teaching undergrads. After getting my master's degree, I decided to take a degree in this field. I did it at Vrije University in Amsterdam. Since then, I kept upgrading my skills.

I looked for a job in the GIS field since 2014 with no success. I got rejected many times because I didn't have experience. If there were qualified jobs, I couldn't pursue them because I would need to relocate.

Despite many rejections, even though it worried me at certain times, I never give up.

Then I took a break. I forget everything I learned or dreamed and searched in another direction. I started from scratch. I explored my hobbies; reading and writing. Then I started a Facebook page for book reviews.

I always dreamt of having my book that would help people. All of a sudden, I got an idea to create a book for girls to help them know their worth and raise their self-esteem. And I did it!

My book was published, and my message was delivered exactly as I wished. Achieving my goal made me get back to my track, my first goal with more energy and enthusiasm."

Asmaa asked me if I would like to support her in this campaign and I said "Yes". This is the power of creation. One step towards creation allows you to do more. Once you create, you develop the habit of turning your ideas to reality. You see results, and it multiplies.

Like me and Asmaa, you too can experience multiplying your creativity. And as you team up with other creators, you will be surprised to see yourself creating things more significant than yourself.

4. Your Creative Work will outlive you

Everything you do today will be part of your history someday. By allowing yourself to move into creative flow, you will be surprised to see yourself creating things you could never imagine.

These creations leave a mark and your legacy that travels across generations. Even though your time in this life is temporary, your legacy will last forever.

> *Please think about your legacy because*
> *you are writing it every day.*
> *- Gary Vaynerchuk*

I like how Gary challenged us with this quote. We do not build legacies in a day. We create them across a lifetime, and they outlive us.

What kind of legacy are you creating now? Is it temporary or are you creating a legacy that will outlive you?

As you look back across your lifetime, what will your life have stood for?

This reminds me of a conversation I had with one of my previous managers. I told her I'm pursuing writing and creating things and experiences according to my priorities and values in life.

She said, "I'm glad you're working on it now. When someone passes away, I don't think they want to be remembered as a good employee. People will forget those projects you delivered, the software you tested, and other things that stressed you at work. In your eulogy, you want to be someone who lived to the fullest and made significant contributions to your family and others."

Isn't that what all of us should strive to do?

Would it be great to create a legacy that impacts the world and the next generations to come and not limit yourself to where you are now?

Do not put on hold the things that matter most to you. Every single step you do should be one step closer to living life to your full potential. Tap into your creativity. Take small steps daily. If you do this consistently, you'll see the path to create your lasting legacy.

> *Get a bigger world and allow yourself to grow. Don't settle in the world you build because it's comfortable. - John Maxwell*

ACTION CHALLENGE:

If you would not be forgotten as soon as you are dead, either write something worth reading or do something worth writing.
- Benjamin Franklin

What do you want to create today?
What will you do to get started?
If you can't think of any but want to tap into your creativity, try this.
Find a notebook or sketchpad and get started. Start using your other hand. Doing something with your left side when you usually use your right hand (or the other way around) wakes up your brain.
Draw a leaf, flower, anything you can think of, and then start writing words, a paragraph. Observe the strokes, shapes, words you used.

INSPIRATIONAL REFLECTION

MY DISABILITY BECOMES A UNIQUE OPPORTUNITY

Need inspiration to create because you lack the resources you need?

Read on about the life story of a man who was born without arms or legs and is now a bestselling author, motivational speaker, philanthropist, and founder of the non-profit organization Life Without Limbs.

Nick Vujicic was born in 1982 in Melbourne, Australia. He was born with a rare congenital disorder known as Phocomelia, which is characterized by the absence of legs and arms. The doctors didn't find any reason why that happened. Although born without arms and legs, he was a very healthy baby.

Growing up, his lack of limbs made him a target for school bullies, and he fell into severe depression. At the age of eight, he contemplated suicide. At ten, he tried to drown himself in a bathtub, but his love for his parents prevented him from following through.

For years, Nick prayed very hard that God would give him arms and legs. However, a critical turning point in his faith came when his mother showed him a newspaper article about a man dealing with a severe disability. He realized others suffered too and began to embrace his lack of limbs.

After that, Nick gradually figured out how to live a full life without limbs, adapting many of the daily skills limbed people accomplish without thinking. He writes with two toes on his left foot and a special grip that slides onto his big toe. He knows how to use a computer and can type up to

45 words per minute using the "heel and toe" method. He has also learned to throw tennis balls, play drum pedals, get a glass of water, comb his hair, brush his teeth, answer the phone and shave, in addition to participating in golf, swimming, and even sky-diving.

Nick believed his purpose was to become a motivational speaker, yet he had no experience, no networks, and no resources. He started calling schools and offering to speak about bullying, dreaming big, and never giving up. He received 52 rejections, but after that, a school finally said yes, and offered him $50. He was ecstatic, then realized it would take almost three hours to drive just to get to the school. He asked his brother to drive him there and offered him the $50. As it turned out, Nick spoke to only ten students for five minutes. He felt foolish after five hours of driving for five-minutes of speaking. But the week after that, his phone started ringing. Many schools asked him to come and share his story. The rest was history. Today, Nick receives around 35000 speaking requests a year. With his humor, faith, and deep and sincere empathy for other human beings, Nick Vujicic has genuinely earned the title of being one of the most inspirational and motivational speakers in the world today.

"I love my life because I've seen my purpose."

Nick Vujicic was born without arms or legs. Despite the many challenges he experienced when he was growing up, his faith in God, the love from his family, and his positive attitude made him conquer them all. He found his purpose and embraced it. The result, he creates his best life and continues creating significance in the lives of others. His disability became an opportunity to inspire many of us who think we lack resources to create the things and life we want.

If Nick can create his best life, you can too. Like Nick, you may have encountered difficult times in your journey. Whether you think it is the lowest point of your life or feeling complacent at this moment, if you are afraid to face the reality that you have resources but are not using them well, you still have time to change things. That time is now. Create your best life now.

LAYING A FOUNDATION FOR CREATIVITY

LET GO TO CREATE

> *We can't be afraid of change. You may feel
> very secure in the pond that you are in,
> but if you never venture out of it, you will
> never know that there is such a thing as an
> ocean, a sea. Holding onto something that
> is good for you now, may be the very reason
> why you don't have something better.*
> *— C. JoyBell C.*

Are you struggling with the baggage you carry in life? Does your past keep coming back to haunt you? Who are you when no one is around?

The majority of us travel through life with baggage. It is like a suitcase we carry that we keep stuffing up until one day, we can't close it anymore, and it starts spilling out in all aspects of our lives.

How much longer do you want to carry your baggage?

You could keep on going with a heavy heart until it explodes. Over time, it affects your creativity. Instead of creating the life that brings out the best in you, you'll end up taking the safest route just to escape from reality.

If you're still struggling from your past and in pain, even if I can't see you; my heart is with you. Because when you are deeply hurt, no one could console you. Inner burdens make our paths a little more challenging to travel. But knowing what baggage you are carrying can help you navigate the road better.

The good news is, you have options to be free from your past. As Rick Warren said, you don't have to be a prisoner of your past. Unless you let go, it will continue to control you. Let go to create space for creativity.

> ***You are the product of your past, but you don't have to be a prisoner.***
> *- Rick Warren*

INNER BURDENS

As you read this chapter, I encourage you to go through all the baggage in your life. Here are some examples of the burdens we carry as we go through life:

1. Your Past

Most of our past burdens come from our childhood. Emotional pain and trauma from youth can haunt us well into adulthood, even being passed across generations.

You were a victim when you were a little child. You were helpless and couldn't do much. When you reach adulthood, you have a choice, to remain a victim of your past or be a creator of the life you deserve to have.

Like a past relationship with people we once trusted and ended up hurting us. How could others betray you despite the kindness you've shown? After many tears, arguments, pain, and anger you experienced, the answer remains unknown.

One thing is real. You can't go back to the past to redo what happened, but you can learn from it and make it better for your present. All you have is today.

When you finally understand that and accept it in your heart that the past is the past, then you'll be able to let go.

If you are still struggling, hold on there. Keep going. If you can't walk, consider crawling. Each step you take to live will lead you to light. But remember to focus on the bright side of life as you take each step.

2. Limiting Negative Beliefs

Everything that you need to create whatever you want is already within you. If you let go of the negativity that's coming from others or yourself, you will create a life experience full of freedom, flow, and fun.

NEGATIVITY COMING FROM OTHERS

When you create and live intentionally, there will be people that say things against you or will not support what you do. Sometimes, these are the people closest to our hearts.

Remember, people who want you to be at your best want you to reach your best. So don't give them any of your time or energy they don't deserve. If you try to convert them to be your supporter or defend yourself when negative feedback comes to you, it will drain more of your energy and just break your heart.

Let them be them. Don't convert them to be your supporters. As Steve Harvey said, "I realized that I have to stop sharing my million-dollar dreams with hundred-dollar people."

Focus on creating the vision that God, your Creator, has given to you. As you take action to create your best life, don't rely on anyone else to provide this momentum for you.

> *You are born to live to the*
> *fullness of your potential.*

You are important and exist for a reason. Creating a change sometimes feels like a burden because it sets you apart from others. But keep going. Later, everything will make more sense, and you will realize, each step you take toward these changes makes you great.

NEGATIVITY COMING FROM YOURSELF

Negative self-talk is something that most of us experience from time to time, and it comes in many forms. It pulls you down and creates significant stress. It gives you negative energy that can radiate throughout your life and flow to the people around you.

Entertaining these thoughts produces a limiting belief that could stop you from rising to your full potential. Some limiting beliefs are:

- I'm not creative
- I don't have time

- I am just...
- I don't have the resources
- I'm too busy

Negative self-talk creates FEAR. To reduce negative self-talk, continue to apply awareness to your life. As covered in an earlier chapter, focusing on fear leads to avoidance. Remember, your thoughts and feelings aren't always reality.

3. Control

As Lao Tzu said, "When I let go of what I am, I become what I might be." You need to let go of too much control if you want to release the creativity in you. Overthinking, over-analyzing, or striving for perfection will prevent you from activating the creative flow. It restricts your thoughts, motions, and connections with everything around you.

As you let go, the creative process will flow. You'll be surprised where it could take you. Let go of your control to fulfill your creative potential.

How are you living your life?

Are you creating a life you enjoy or one you just endure?

ACTION CHALLENGE:

If you're tired of going through the motion, ready to turn your ideas into reality, and create the life you want, I can help you. Start by taking the time to reflect below and make your vision a reality.

What are the things you want to do?

What's stopping you from starting?

If you are thinking of delaying things till your retirement, when the kids are older, when you have saved enough money if the perfect time comes, what if it doesn't come? What if the only time you have is NOW?

BREAKING OUT OF SURVIVAL MODE

*The habits you created to survive will no
longer serve you when it's time to thrive.*
Ebonee Davis

Creativity is the freest form of self-expression. It begins with wondering and questioning, like a young child eager to learn and curious by nature. They are perfect explorers and not afraid to ask anything. As Albert Einstein said, "To stimulate creativity, one must develop the childlike inclination for play."

According to Harvard-based child psychologist Paul Harris, a child asks around 40,000 questions between the ages of two and five. He described it as "a series of complex mental maneuvers." It starts with knowing what they don't know and longing for an explanation. The asking of a question also shows that the child understands there are various answers.

Children can produce a range of ideas — freely, generously, and without an inner critic taking notes. If ideas don't work, they move on to the next one.

The thing is, all grown-ups were once children, and naturally creative. But as we get older and grow accustomed to life's demands and responsibilities, our connection to our creative roots weaken. At some point in our lives, we become afraid to ask questions. We develop reservations and become scared that certain things sound stupid when we ask.

We view a mistake as a failure instead of learning from it as part of the creative process. We adapt to social norms and accepted ways of thinking, making us more effective with people and society. We build walls to avoid vulnerability.

As a result, the creativity flow stops moving towards the direction it should. We see fewer opportunities around us. We stop creating and are just surviving.

The good news is, creativity is an innate quality that everyone possesses. But for you to move forward, it is essential to understand the things you do that prevent your growth.

> *The habits you created to survive will no longer serve when it's time to thrive.*
> *- Ebonee Davis*

GET OUT OF SURVIVAL MODE TO CREATE YOUR BEST LIFE

Below is the list of common things people do that kills creativity. To break out of the survival mode, identify the ones you can resonate with:

1. Playing it too safe - You Stay Within Your Comfort Zone

Have you stopped caring for your growth and trade time for money?

Have you convinced yourself to live a life that is comfortable and easy?

If you allow yourself to dwell in your comfort zone for a long time, you can't get past the status quo, a life that is 'good enough.' You get comfortable. As a result, you don't make the trade-offs for growth.

One danger of living in a mediocre life for too long is that it can make a person unteachable. Many people stayed in the same jobs, relationships, places they don't like, because of the belief that where they are or what they have is good enough. Their previous success and achievements became a reason to discontinue their growth. They trade innovation and growth for a formula that they follow time after time.

If you want to keep growing, you need to keep making trades. Why? Because the skills you have to be where you are probably not the same skills you need to be where you want to be.

This is so true today when everything is changing rapidly. A few years ago, Zoom didn't exist. Now, think about how it is becoming a primary tool we use to communicate in our businesses and culture, especially when we faced challenges during the the COVID-19 pandemic.

No matter where you are in life, there is always space for growth. But remember, each choice you make will cost you.

> *The price of anything is the amount*
> *of life you exchange for it.*
> *Henry David Thoreau*

Playing it too safe and creativity don't go together. To nurture your creativity, you need to keep learning and growing. To grow, you trade part of your life to receive something that would bring out the best in you. It will not be easy, but it's essential.

Creative people expose themselves to new ideas and take the time to explore them. Each step taken contributes to your growth.

2. Live unintentionally

Are you too busy with the things that keep you occupied, but not fulfilled? Do you daydream about being somewhere else but never thought of the actions to take to get there?

What separates people from those who create, and the ones wishing, is being intentional. It doesn't mean you have it all figured out; it is choosing to live in a way that is in alignment with your purpose in life. You're not just going through the motions.

How many hours did you spend on entertainment without spending a little time to grow yourself? How many times did you create performance goals for work, but you never did any for yourself?

Every little thing we do, when done consistently, contributes to the power of intangible compounding. Each day is just as important as the next in creating the life we imagined. Start now. Commit yourself to live intentionally.

3. Being close-minded

As Frank Zappa said, "A mind is like a parachute. It doesn't work if it is not open." Closed-minded people are more interested in proving themselves right than in getting the best outcome. Most of the time, they don't ask questions and are not interested in growth. They are not curious about other people's life stories, perspectives, or psychology, and stick to what they believe in.

On the other hand, open-mindedness is equated with positivity and growth. It helps us to take risks, find opportunities, understand others, and manage uncertainty. It also means being receptive to new ideas and willing to consider other perspectives to see if they hold any value.

Examine your habits and asses the areas in your life. Where can you be more open-minded?

When you find yourself being close-minded, acknowledge what's happening and correct it. Don't blame yourself. As soon as you can, find time to reflect on what happened, learn from it, and aim to do better next time.

4. Analysis paralysis

Have you seen yourself spending hours planning, analyzing, evaluating, and ended up not taking action? In short, you got lost in overthinking and felt paralyzed to move to the next step.

If so, you're not alone. Analysis paralysis is a common trap for many of us. To avoid analysis paralysis, differentiate decisions by importance, break them into smaller steps, and put a healthy amount of pressure on yourself and your team to decide.

5. Learning without Doing

Learning is good, but at some point, you need to take action. Author and speaker, Darren Hardy said in his book, The Compound Effect, "Knowledge uninvested is wasted."

How many books do you need to read to learn to start? How many motivational videos and speakers do you need to see before taking action?

Start with what you have now. Look around. Your knowledge will keep you in the same place, and it's your action that will bring you further.

6. Relying on the experts alone

Have you seen yourself often seeking approval from experts before taking any action?

Although working with experts like coaches, trainers and mentors can help you have clarity and will save you tons of time, remember that whatever you do, it's your responsibility. It is not because some experts told you so.

Learn from others, respect their expertise, follow what makes sense, but keep your identity.

Your life is your signature creation.
It is your duty to live true to
yourself, with authenticity.

If you can identify yourself above, that's a good start. Remember, you cannot change what you refuse to confront. Knowing what's standing in your way, whatever makes you feel stuck, can serve as a guideline for the areas you need to focus on next. You're on your way!

In the later chapters, we will cover how you can nurture your creativity, and be as creative as a child again.

ACTION CHALLENGE:

Pick up a pen and start jotting down your ideas. You can start writing, *"I'm creative! I'm creative, I'm creative"*.

Start doodling. Start baking, woodworking, or anything that allows you to create.

Every day is an opportunity to build good habits toward creativity that will serve you or create habits that steal your productivity. Choose wisely.

INSPIRATIONAL REFLECTION

CREATIVITY IN THE MARKET PLACE: BRINGING DATA TO LIFE

Several years ago I met Emily Sy, a very smart, soft-spoken, yet very humble woman in Singapore. She faced many challenges during her journey in life, but despite all her fears, her faith in God and herself prevails.

The recent story she shared about using faith and creativity is from her workplace. Emily has worked in a Project Management Office for the past four years. I asked her if she still enjoys what she does and how she continues to apply creativity at work.

She said, "My job can get very technical and sometimes boring because you deal with lots of data. Since I started, my presentation has transformed significantly. From being plain and sometimes confusing to very engaging and direct to the point. Every time I present something, I make sure it's easy-to-understand and visually stimulating."

THOUGHTS ABOUT CREATING

"When I'm working on complex data, Steve Jobs is one of my inspirations. Focus on simplicity. But in my journey, I experienced many cringes-worthy moments. At those times, I had to stop for a bit and reflect on what happened. I assessed how I could do well next time."

Focus and simplicity. Simple can be harder than complex: You have to work hard to get your thinking clean to make it simple. But it's worth it in the end because once you get there, you can move mountains.
— Steve Jobs

"I invested in myself and that that leveled up my performance. I took a course about Data Storytelling that equipped me to present more clearly and engagingly. I learned about effective strategies and different tools to transform confusing and plain data into beautiful and edgy work. It equipped me to bring data to life.

Aside from my daily tasks, I manage team events as well. The goal is to promote collaboration and teamwork. These activities help to break the silo mentality in the workplace. Every time we do it, fresh ideas come out, and the team gets closer to one another.

I enjoy what I do. I faced many challenges along the road, but I like it; it brings out the best in me. Sometimes, I even have a eureka moment about how to deal with different situations.

After all the hard work and going through the process, there is fulfillment. I discovered more about myself. What makes my heart rejoice more is to witness the impact on others because of what I'm doing. Everyone learned and enjoyed the process. Even if I get exhausted, I know it's worth it!"

Emily Sy on conducting engaging presentation at work

VULNERABILITY IN CREATIVITY

"Most of the time, I prefer to be an observer rather than the main speaker. When I step into the meetings, I still feel scared and vulnerable. I don't have all the answers, but I know that someone's got my back. I give my best in each presentation.

I do my part, but I also lean on God to provide me with the wisdom and strength I need. I pray and let his grace flow into me. I ask, Lord, how do you want me to design this? Just one touch of creativity from you is all it takes for me to do these things.

I started with very few ideas and no clarity at all, but I knew that He was with me. Then, as I connected to my creator, my God, I would suddenly feel the creative flow. I would start planning, drawing, or visualizing. I think that's what creativity is all about. Expressing yourself and tapping into your source."

HOW TO PROCEED IF YOU'RE CONTEMPLATING STARTING ON YOUR IDEA?

"First, allow yourself to make mistakes. As John Maxwell said, fail forward. If you make mistakes, learn from them and pick yourself up, then move on. Because that's how you will grow. It's okay to make mistakes but don't make the same mistake again.

Second, allow God to hold on to you. It will not be a smooth process, but with him, you'll find wisdom, peace, and direction."

> *Let your light so shine before men, that they may see your good works, and glorify your Father which is in heaven.*
> *- Matthew 5:16 (KJV)*

Like Emily, you too can find a unique story in whatever you do and bring it to life. **No matter how dull the situation you are in, there is a space for creativity to add colors to life.**

As you tap into your creativity, you will discover something new every day. New ideas or things that you never knew existed. When you take one step forward, it will unleash your inner strength and will push you beyond your limit. Even though you face challenges, you focus on solutions. You keep growing and becoming a better version of you.

SET GOALS, NOT WISHES

*Greater things never came
from comfort zones
- author unknown*

What do you want in life? What do you love? What fulfills you?

Michael Jordan said "Some people want it to happen, some wish it would happen, others make it happen." Do you have a wish, or desire to turn what you want into reality?

Understanding the difference between a wish and a goal can transform the result you're looking for. In reality, there is no magic wand you can wave that gives you your wants instantly. If you want it, you have to work for it.

Goals are powerful tools for change. They give you something to aim for and map out the route for a better future. It is a call to action and can provide forward momentum. It is manageable and attainable.

A goal without a plan is a wish. They are idle fantasies detached from reality. They can be pleasant diversions and may give temporary relief from the demands of the real world, but are passive, and don't motivate you to take action. When you are wishing, you are fantasizing.

Wishes are vague, ambiguous, and not constructive. Goals are clear, specific, and actionable.

For example, "I wish I could lose weight. I wish I didn't have to go to work. I wish I had the answers for the next exam. I wish I had a better memory. I wish I was a millionaire. I wish I could go back in time and do it differently. I wish I had more confidence. I wish I had the resources to make my dreams come true."

Creators don't sit down and say, "I wish I could make something…" They focus on thinking about what to do at a specific moment. They don't hope for someone to provide the resources. Creators identify what they want and find the resources. In short, to create what you want is not something you wish for, but something you do.

Instead of wishing for the things you want to accomplish, ask yourself what you can do to make it happen. Such as, what can I do to lose weight? What can I do to attain financial freedom? What can I do to gain more confidence? What can I do to create my best life?

Once you've identified the things you can do, the things you have control over, convert your wish into a goal. This will help you focus on execution.

> *Wishes are like dreams, they*
> *can motivate you, but goals*
> *can change your life.*

INSPIRATIONAL REFLECTION

CREATING A BUSINESS WITH A BIGGER PURPOSE

When it comes to turning business dreams into goals, Marlon Mancego is a legend. He started several businesses when he was in high school. He is constantly building, creating, mentoring, and supporting others who want to pursue the same path.

Marlon grew up in a family of entrepreneurs. As he watched his parents and siblings managing different businesses, he knew there was only one way to live where he could maximize his full potential. To be an entrepreneur himself.

But the road to success is not always easy to navigate. Marlon's family migrated to other countries and sold everything. Sponsorship for siblings over 18 years of age wasn't possible, so he was left alone.

Determined to reunite with them again, he explored the surrounding opportunities. His journey lead him to the birth of his business that changed his life and transformed others too. Here's his story.

"I started my first business venture in college. My brother managed an automotive bodyshop and he handed it over to me. My family's business was in school bus servicing. Vehicles need maintenance and repairs almost every day, so having a garage was a no brainer. I managed it for years.

Then I went to Singapore to visit a few friends. I fell in love with the place. So, I did my research, asked friends about moving there, and then I worked towards it. Eventually, I found a job, but during that time, I knew my long-term goal was to manage a business of my own."

Marlon had a full-time job in Singapore when he started working in Architectural 3D Visualization. As he wanted to run his own business, he created a plan to work towards it. His determination kept him focused on taking one step forward to fulfill his goal despite being clueless on his new venture.

He worked in architectural and engineering companies to understand the ins and outs of the business. While working full time, he spent hours at night to consistently build up his business. As time went by, his earnings from his side hustle exceeded his full-time job income. That was his sign to quit his job and to focus on his side hustle.

"I had to take a conservative approach before I took a leap to do it fulltime. When that time came, it felt like I was in total control of my life. It felt good. No more deadlines, I felt fulfilled. I created it from scratch, and now it's a stable business that provides not only for my family, but my staff too."

"My business consistently puts food on the table not only for myself but also for my staff and everyone around me. As I scale up, it will get better. I help my fellow countrymen reach out to talented individuals and provide better opportunities for them. Focusing on this purpose keeps me going, not the business. It's like my fuel."

———〰———

Like many of us, everything started with an idea. For Marlon, it was a desire to reunite with his family, create a business, and maximize his full potential. That desire, when turned into a goal, allowed him to take action to fulfill it.

Now, Marlon happily lives in Canada and is reunited with his family. He runs his own business from the comfort of his home-office and provides job opportunities to individuals from his homeland.

IN TURNING YOUR BUSINESS DREAM INTO A REALITY

Marlon Mancego is the founder and CEO of Silvercouch, a leading 3D visualization company specializing in high-end quality renderings for residential and commercial spaces. Applying the principles he learned by doing things with integrity and valuing the relationship with his clients and staff, Silvercouch is known for providing exceptional quality 3D rendering image and excellent service.

Throughout his journey, he met many people who wanted to have their own business but never got started. Marlon continues to share his experience with others. If you are contemplating starting your own business, it's worth following in his footsteps.

"In business, the opposite of doing is not a failure, but FEAR. Failure is part of the process. Think about it; we spend almost 15 years or more in school in preparation to get a job. In business, we don't have the luxury of time to learn everything before we start. My advice, do your part, then take a leap! If you fail, get up and stay on course.

Remember, there's no universal method for a successful business, but there's a universal attitude, discipline, and drive to succeed. Also, don't rely on others to get started, like looking for a mentor, coach, etc., because sometimes it as an excuse not to step up. People have limitations, and if you're relying on them at all times, you'll be losing your own identity and miss other perspectives.

No one has all the answers, and not all of us can afford a mentor. Instead of looking for a mentor, look for your heroes or someone already successful in your chosen field. With social media available to us, you can easily access these resources. It's free. Widen your horizon.

Start watching TED talks, read books, and get any videos that could help in your chosen journey.

Successful people leave tracks and clues to how they made it. They do certain things, then do it again–that's excellence, that's perfection. Pick up those pieces to build your puzzle, then start. Join and attend business networks, join meetups. Use that voice in your head as a compass to help you navigate and follow a path to starting your business.

If you found a mentor that could support you, that's great. If you don't have one, don't let it stop you from getting started. Keep an open mind and look around you. Vast information is available for you to start and build your business."

> *Being challenged in life is inevitable;*
> *being defeated is optional.*
> Roger Crawford

"One challenge I face, like in any other business, is when clients don't pay on time. You have overhead expenses and obligations to your staff, who are the soul of your business.

When you encounter challenges, do what's needed and keep going. Always think that your wings are too wide to be dragged down by problems. If you remain focused on your purpose, you will learn how to maneuver through difficult times without having your business crushed. You will face challenges along the way. It's good for you. It strengthens you and makes you smarter about what you do."

TOP QUALITIES TO TURN YOUR BUSINESS IDEA INTO REALITY

"Integrity because people should be able to trust you in whatever business or service you give. Have a good character because it is seen even when no one is looking.

Be sociable to speed up your business. Surround yourself with people. Consider networking with like-minded individuals.

Develop an entrepreneurial vision and mindset. Seeing things from a new angle leads to a mindset strong in creation and innovation. We can develop this mindset. You will see the problems you want to solve and other sources of innovation in that same product, but you will interpret it in a different way."

THOUGHTS IN HAVING A PASSION FOR STARTING A BUSINESS

"I believe that passion can be developed along the way, so it's better to seek opportunities first and test it out. In my experience, if I had gone after my passions, I would not have gone into 3D rendering business. But now, that I'm working on it, I've been following people who are into 3D rendering. I keep myself up to date in this world, and I would say, I am now very passionate about it.

Some people succeed in running a business because of passion. But I would say, it's better to focus on opportunities around you and not limit yourself. Do your research, test it out, test the market, see what we need out there, and learn from it if it doesn't work."

For Marlon, all the hard work paid off. The fulfillment is not just about having his own business; it's the overall growth he experiences. The result, he is living a life he designed, maximizing his full potential to glorify his Creator, God, and creating significance in the lives of others.

BORN TO THRIVE

Jet Capinpin is an immigrant from the Philippines and is now running a profitable real estate business which involves rental property management, construction and investments in Canada.

I asked Jet how he created his business and here's his story:

"It was one of those AHA moments. My profession is in IT. I've always been in front of a computer. I never worked on a house project before.

In 2006, I moved to Canada, then my wife joined me after a year and we bought our first house. With all the expenses accumulated during our transition period, our savings shrunk. Knowing that we had to remain frugal with all the expenses, we purchased the cheapest house we could afford.

Each time we got our paychecks, we purchased tools and materials to make the place nicer. We painted the house and renovated it. Three years later, we sold it. We earned

$38,000.00 gross profit. We were ecstatic! I looked at my wife and said, "We can do this!"

We put our profit towards our second house, and then the rest was history. We continued to purchase real estate properties. We buy and sell, renovate, and rent most of the properties. Now, we give our investors an 8-18% return, provide people creative housing solutions, and help homeowners prevent foreclosures.

When it comes to how my entrepreneurial mindset started, I tell them jokingly; I was made in the Philippines, a Filipino mother, and a Chinese father. I wasn't entirely sure, but I think the genes could be a huge factor. Chinese people are known for being business-minded and hardworking. We know Filipinos for creativity and perseverance."

THOUGHTS ABOUT MAKING THINGS HAPPEN

"I like what Jay Shetty said about having the mind as the most expensive real estate in the world. I don't do things just because everybody else does. I need to see the logic and rationale before I do it. I believe there are better ways and always room for improvement. If the room is dark, I would rather look for the matches and light the candle than whine all day and curse the darkness."

> *The most expensive real estate in the world is your MIND.*
> *- Jay Shetty*

"Life is too short and fragile to be complicated or boring. We all have one shot in this world, and that's it. When we die, our game is over. You can't reboot and start your life all over again. You have one shot, and that's it. Live a fun and meaningful life. Don't just go with the flow. Even a dead fish can go with the flow."

IN STARTING A BUSINESS WHILE WORKING...

"Right now, I am still working full time for the government and doing my real estate business on the side. Now that my wife just finished her nursing degree, maybe I can allocate more time to my real estate business.

I often tell my real estate students, don't quit your job unless it costs you money or you're no longer growing. Don't start a business when you desperately need to have one; it will not work. Start a business when you don't need it.

Keeping my day job while doing real estate is like having the best of both worlds in terms of mortgage financing as we get access to more lenders."

VULNERABILITY IN CREATIVITY

"You need to let go of your shield and put your guard down to let the creativity flow. If you are comfortable, where everything you need is available to you, nothing will push you to grow.

Humans are emotional creatures by nature. We need to feel something to trigger another thing. When we allow ourselves to experience pain and become vulnerable, it helps us realize what we need and ultimately, what matters most.

In my case, I think when I moved to Canada was the point of my life where I was most vulnerable. When you migrate to another country as a child with your parents, it can be hard. Moving to another country as an adult, with many more responsibilities to take on, in my experience, is like suicide.

I felt I was on my own. When you're starting, you have no friends, no family, and no place to go. Yet life must move on, or you just give up. I had to familiarize myself with the culture and learned different things. I had to find a job, a place to stay, a vehicle to use, and take care of my bills.

While struggling to settle down in my new life, I also had to support my family back home. It was a tough journey. It wasn't just stepping out of my comfort zone. I felt it stripped me of my whole being.

People asked me how's life as an immigrant. I said, everything you learn in the first 18 years of your life, you need to learn in six months or fewer to survive.

When you hit rock bottom, all unnecessary things are gone. Everything becomes clear. I see it as burning your boats behind you. When you have nothing to go back to, it is either you win or you die. No other way.

I'm building something bigger than myself-for my children and the next generation. I think that's when we live life. When we look past ourselves, think of what we can do for others, beyond yourself, beyond your family. You have a higher purpose of waking up for in the morning."

YOUR BIGGEST CHALLENGE IS YOURSELF

"Most of the time, we look outside and blame others. The reality is – it is us. It is either we block or expedite our success. It is difficult to manage our selves. If we all knew how to manage ourselves well, the world would be a better place.

During challenging times, I go back to my "why." Why am I here? Why do I do what I do? The two most important days in our lives are the day you were born and the day you found out your 'why'. Find your WHY. Once you know and understand your WHY, no one can stop you."

WORDS OF WISDOM

For you to create and be a change-maker, you need to know yourself. Don't stop reaching for your dreams and help others achieve theirs.

For Jet, moving to Canada was the most difficult decision he ever made, but he would do it again. The hardships he experienced allowed him to grow and become the strong man he is now. He learned not to depend on anyone, but only on his Creator, God, alone.

Like Marlon and Jet, you have a Creator inside of you. If you want to create a business, YOU have everything you need to turn your dream business into reality. But you have to see and believe it first; then as you do, take action towards it and set a realistic approach to achieve it.

ACTION CHALLENGE:

Reflect on what you want to do at this point in your life. What do you love? What fulfills you?

Set an actionable plan to turn your desires into goals. You can split them into short term, medium-term and long term goals. Begin working on the plan to successfully accomplish these goals.

You can download some templates I created for you in **free resources**.

8

DEVELOP THE CREATIVITY WITHIN YOU

*What is necessary to change a person is
to change his awareness of himself.*
- Abraham Maslow

Creativity is about finding new ways to solve problems and approach different situations. To boost your creativity, it is important to square away a few key things first. This helps to develop the foundation to decide and move forward.

ENABLE THE GROWTH MINDSET

Why do some people succeed and live a fulfilled life?

Why do others just drag themselves through life daily to survive?

What makes some turn ideas into reality and others to remain as dreamers?

Mindset is a big underlying factor to all these questions. It plays a critical role in how you cope with life's challenges. It is your mental attitude that is shaped by your life experiences, environment, education, and the ideas and beliefs you have absorbed throughout your life. It is your way of thinking.

Your mindset is responsible for how you interpret and react to what happens to you and around you.

Carol Dweck, a researcher on human motivation and author of the book <u>Mindset</u>, identified two types of mindsets: a fixed and a growth.

In a fixed mindset, people believe you either are or aren't good at something, based on your inherent nature. You cannot change it because it's who you are. They believe that talent alone leads to success, and it does not require effort.

In a growth mindset, people have an underlying belief that anyone can be good at anything. You believe that your abilities are because of your actions.

Having a fixed mindset keeps you in your comfort zone. Until you're able to reprogram your mind to allow success, abundance, and creativity to flow to you, nothing will change. No matter how many books you've read, conferences you've gone to, motivational videos you've watched, coaches and mentors you've talked to, you will get the same result.

And that brings us to the question, how can you reprogram your mindset to attain greater things?

The key is to understand what kind of mindset you possess right now and develop the growth mindset inside you.

We all have a mixture of fixed and growth mindset inside us. It evolves with our experience. To remain in a growth zone, we must identify where we are and cultivate the growth mindset. It is the key to success and a fulfilled life.

Having this mindset will push you to step out of your comfort zone and unlock your creative side. You will stop blaming everybody else and start taking responsibility for your life.

You become open to opportunities around you. You know everyone can develop their abilities through hard work, system or strategies, and help from others. Despite your circumstances, you will learn to ask yourself questions that will bring out the best in you instead of pulling you down.

People with a growth mindset are living a life by design, not by default. They make time to create and focus on creating harmony in life. As a result, they gain clarity on their purpose and fulfillment from what they do.

Many creators are told that they would never amount to anything, but they believe in themselves and that every action can lead them to a better direction. They turn ideas to reality and create the life of their dreams.

The good news is, because mindset results from everything we've learned and been exposed to, we can also unlearn things that are not giving us the results we want. We are capable of training our minds to learn and experience what we truly want in our lives.

If you made it this far reading this chapter, I assume that there is a part of you that is curious. The outcome of what you will learn will depend on you.

To get the maximum benefit from this book, you need to enable a Growth Mindset in you. Training yourself to embrace growth will open up unlimited possibilities.

Here are six of the recommended practices for developing a growth mindset.

1. Practice Curiosity

Ask Questions. Explore. Allow yourself to be amazed and appreciate the beauty of life. Live in wonderment. Keep the child within you alive.

2. Stop seeking approval from others.

Learn to accept yourself for who you are. Practice awareness about why you're seeking approval.

> *When you prioritize approval over learning, you sacrifice your potential for growth.*

Develop a greater sense of self-worth. Keep an open mind but learn to stand for yourself. As you develop this, you will learn to value yourself more. Determined people get approval from themselves first. They never give up and make a difference in the lives of many.

3. Explore different learning approach.

There's no one-size-fits-all model for learning. Some learn by reading alone, others do well when collaborating with others. Some prefer words, others like visuals or both. What works for one person may not work for you. Try different learning strategies.

4. Replace the word "failing" with the word "learning."

When you make a mistake or fall short of a goal, you haven't failed; you've learned.

5. Take ownership over your attitude.

Once you develop a growth mindset, own it. Acknowledge yourself as someone who possesses a growth mentality and be proud to let it guide you throughout your educational career.

6. Be inspired and take action, stop just being entertained.

If being entertained stops you from bringing out the best in you, do something about it. Inspirations and motivations are excellent but it's the action you take that determines where you will go.

IMPROVE YOUR SELF-AWARENESS

Awareness is the ability to recognize and perceive, to feel, or to be mindful of events. It is understanding how you think about, how you respond to, and express feelings about them.

Self-awareness is the ability to see ourselves clearly, to understand who we are and how others see us. We may not always like what we see, but there is a comfort knowing ourselves.

Increasing your awareness will help your creativity emerge. It allows you to predict your reactions and take steps to control negative or unproductive emotions. It will enable you to be in control of your actions to get the outcomes you desire. Where you choose to focus your energy, emotions, personality, and reactions determines where you will end up in life.

Like many other qualities, awareness of our thoughts is not an innate trait. You have to cultivate it if you want to apply it in your life.

Here are some tips to increase your awareness:

1. Look at yourself objectively.

It is the ability to detach yourself from a situation in which you usually react and instead respond in a proactive state to the situation. When you can see yourself objectively, you can learn how to accept yourself and improve yourself.

To get started, ask people who care about you, and have known you for a long time, what they think and feel about you. Encourage them to be honest and reflect on their feedback. If you detach yourself as the receiver of the feedback and position yourself as a third person, you can easily take it constructively.

2. Ask yourself "What" and not why

Tasha Eurich, author of <u>Insight</u>, has spent years researching what it truly means to be self-aware, and in the process, has made a surprising discovery about human perception. In her TED talk, she dissects common misbeliefs about introspective thinking and provides a simple way we can get to know ourselves just a little bit better.

Here's what she explained, "unfortunately, when we ask "Why?" it doesn't lead us towards the truth about ourselves. It leads us away from it.

Researchers have found that no matter how hard we try, we can't excavate our unconscious thoughts, feelings and motives. Because so much is hidden from our conscious awareness, we end up inventing answers that feel true but are often very wrong.

The second reason asking "Why?" is a bad idea, is that it leads us away from our true nature. We like to think of our brains as computers rationally analyzing information and arriving at accurate conclusions. Unfortunately, that's not what happens.

Asking "Why?" creates "alternative facts" and over time, this leads us away from who we really are. It clouds our self-perceptions. So you might wonder if asking "Why?" makes us depressed, over-confident and wrong; it's probably not going to increase our self-awareness.

So if we shouldn't ask "Why?" then what should we ask?" She justified the reasons based on research.

She explained, "We analyzed literally hundreds of pages of transcripts, and we saw a very clear pattern. Although the word "why" appeared less than 150 times, the word "what" appeared more than 1000 times.

Let me give you a few examples. Nathan, a brand manager, got a terrible performance review from his new boss. Instead of asking, "Why are we like oil and water?" He asked, "What can I do to show her I'm the best person for this job?"

It changed everything. People now point to Nathan and his boss as proof that polar opposites can work together.

Sarah, an education leader, was diagnosed with breast cancer in her late 40s. When she asked, "Why me?" she said it felt like a death sentence. So then she asked, "What's most important to me?"

This helped her define what she wanted her life to look like in whatever time she had left. She's now cancer-free and more focused on the relationships that mean the most to her.

Jose, an entertainment industry veteran, hated his job. Instead of getting stuck, what most of us would do, and ask, "Why do I feel so terrible?" he asked, "What are the situations that make me feel terrible, and what do they have in common?"

He quickly realized that he would never be happy in this job, and it gave him the courage to pursue a new and far more fulfilling career path as a wealth manager."

Next time you feel overwhelmed focusing on "why", take a step back and focus on "what needs to be done in the moment". You will be surprised how it will help you to get unstuck and move forward

3. Keep a journal.

Start writing. Write down your thoughts, feelings, reflections, or anything you can think. Aside from increasing your awareness, it will also help you boost your memory, inspire creativity, and relieve stress.

4. Perform daily self-reflection.

Having time alone gives you the space you need to reflect and process.

Self-reflection is like looking into a mirror and describing what you see. It is a way of assessing yourself, your thoughts and actions. To start, set aside a specific time to reflect. Remove any distractions. Start small, like 15 minutes each day. Reflect by asking questions or thinking of events in your life.

Here are some questions you can ask:

- What are the situations that make me feel terrible, and what do they have in common?
- What made you happy when you were a little child?
- What has changed, and why did the changes happen?
- What are the things you are proud of?

- What other things do you want to accomplish?
- What makes you feel sad, happy, or mad?
- What scares you?
- What stops you from doing what you want?

5. Practice meditation or other mindfulness habits.

Meditation is the practice of improving your mindfulness. This is often accomplished by focusing on breathing. You can also find greater clarity from regular moments of reflection. Both practices can be either formal or informal.

The above steps will help you get started improving your self-awareness. But becoming fully self-aware requires help. To develop self-awareness, you need help from others who can see you more clearly than how you see yourself.

The most critical step in the awareness development process is a review of results from the actions taken. It is a process that takes time and repetition. As you've taken the necessary action towards the assessment of your results, you are becoming a better version of yourself.

UNDERSTAND YOUR FEAR

Fear is an emotion induced by perceived danger or threat. It causes physiological changes and ultimately behavioral changes, such as fleeing, hiding, or freezing during perceived traumatic events.

Creativity is letting go,
Fear is holding on.

FEAR will keep you where you are. Awareness of fear will allow you to move forward.

Focusing on Fear is one of the reasons people stop creating. If you dwell on it, it keeps you in a 'SAFETY' place, your comfort zone. Fear leads to avoidance. Avoidance of making any change that will allow you to grow.

FEAR OF DISCOMFORT AND LOSING CONTROL

I followed a group of people who wanted to create things or make changes for several years. Many of them want to create businesses, books, and blogs or start a hobby. Others wanted to do better than they were doing now, to have a better figure, relationship, job, house, car, gadgets, etc. Ultimately, time goes by but nothing changes.

If you want it, why not take action? As I pondered this thought, I realized that many people wanted something without being uncomfortable and without doing the work like:

- Increasing income without upgrading their skills.
- Losing weight without exercising or changing the food eaten
- Wanting to publish a book without spending money and finding time to write
- Attaining financial freedom without saving, investing and multiplying their income
- Trying to achieve goals without working towards them

To get something you want, you have to work for it. *As Thomas Jefferson said, "If you want something you never had, you have to do something you've never done."*

When you're doing something new or outside your comfort zone, you will experience discomfort. Focusing on discomfort activates that Fear of Losing Control. And when this happens, you immediately stop taking action.

There is no guaranteed way to get the results you want, nor to have control over the situation or other people's perception of you. It will always be uncomfortable. Lisa Nichols explained it so well in her book, <u>Abundance Now</u> and it's worth quoting. She wrote:

> *"Because we fear other people's perception of us—and because we unconsciously suffer from our own fear of failure—we actually become more committed to looking good than to succeeding. We would rather stay stagnant and look good in mediocrity than risk making a fool of ourselves reaching for extraordinary. Even worse, many of us spend lots of time, money, and energy being "busy" when what we're really doing is standing still. While we may be in motion, we're doing the wrong things. Our subconscious mind is silently keeping us from taking those actions that will truly help us meet our goals. There's no forward movement toward our future."*
> *- Lisa Nichols*

The simple act of being uncomfortable can solve many of our problems. As you become comfortable being uncomfortable, it can help you accomplish many things in life, probably more than you can imagine.

This is one major skill successful people have applied in their lives. The FEAR of staying where they are is higher than the fear of being uncomfortable. So they take risks. They equipped themselves, embraced the situation, and acknowledged that fear exists, but they took action.

FEAR is good for you if you know how to deal with it. And that's where awareness comes in again. Acknowledge fear, but don't focus on it. Instead focus on what you want to accomplish. It's only when you embrace fear that you can take the first step forward.

This is a discovery I made a few years back when I tried to change my life. I had to step back to reassess my priorities. The fear of staying where I was has given me more pain than the fear of stepping into the unknown. It was the fear of not achieving my full potential, of not creating the life and experience I wanted.

WHAT ACTION ARE YOU TAKING?

You may have had the burning desire to create something for a very long time, but you're trapped in avoidance mode.

Don't let fear kill your dreams before you even get started.

Doing things that scare you is one of the best ways to grow. Remember, the only way you will know for sure is to step forward. Check out the <u>additional resources</u> available for you to support you in moving forward.

If you can learn to manage your fear, your life will have almost no limits. There's no better skill to learn.

ACTIVATE YOUR FAITH

As your desire to create increases I encourage you to boost your Faith to step into the unknown and take action to move towards Creativity.

What is Faith?

FAITH is taking action and having confidence that each step takes you closer to your goal. Even if you are clueless about how things will work, while understanding your imperfections, you still take one step forward.

In my journey, I met many people who have faith in God but are lacking faith in their own selves. To create, you need to embrace change, taking one step at a time towards creating. Even if the outcome is unknown, the journey of allowing yourself to go through the creative process will reveal many discoveries about yourself and life.

Faith without action is dead. – James 2:17

No matter how big your faith in God, or whatever you believe in, if you don't have faith in yourself and do your part, you'll remain in your dream land.

Have faith in yourself and your Creator will be with you on the journey. You are strong enough to handle challenges, but you'll never know until you step into the unknown. You can pull things through despite your imperfections.

Once you apply this principle in your life, you will realign your actions to meet the desires of your heart. When alignment begins, the creative flow will kick in. At the right time, it will all come together.

You've got this, YOU are enough to create.

ACTION CHALLENGE:

We've come a long way together. This chapter has given you what you need to develop the creative mindset within you, but what you do with these skills/information is entirely up to you.

When you stop reading this chapter, you can feel you've learned something, get inspired and go on as you normally to.

I encourage you to take a break and spend some time to reflect on each area you need to develop and work towards it. It will help you to digest the material and start taking actions on what's really important.

LET GO AND CREATE

INSPIRATIONAL REFLECTION

CREATIVE LIVING – SPARK JOY IN YOUR LIFE

Elizabeth Gilbert was born in Waterbury, Connecticut in 1969, and grew up on a small family Christmas tree farm. She attended New York University, where she studied political science by day and worked on her short stories by night. After college, she spent several years traveling around the country, working in bars, diners, and ranches, collecting experiences to transform into fiction.

She is best known for her 2006 memoir Eat, Pray, Love, which later turned into a movie starring Julia Roberts. In one of her other best-selling books, Big Magic, she asked the question, "What is creative living?"

Her answer, "Any life that is driven more strongly by curiosity than by fear." She also shared the story of her friend who applied creative living in her life that is worth quoting. Here's what she wrote:

"This, I believe, is the central question upon which all creative living hinges: **Do you have the courage to bring forth the treasures that are hidden within you?**

Look, I don't know what's hidden within you. You may barely know, although I suspect you've caught glimpses. I don't know your capacities, your aspirations, your longings, your secret talents. But surely something wonderful is sheltered inside you. I say this with all confidence because I happen to believe we are all walking repositories of buried treasure. I believe this is one of the oldest and most generous tricks the universe plays on us human beings, both for its own amusement and for ours: The universe buries strange jewels deep within us all, and then stands back to see if we can find them.

The hunt to uncover those jewels—that's creative living. The courage to go on that hunt in the first place—that's what separates a mundane existence from a more enchanted one.

The often surprising results of that hunt—that's what I call Big Magic.

When I talk about "creative living" here, please understand that I am not necessarily talking about pursuing a life that is professionally or exclusively devoted to the arts. When I refer to "creative living," I am speaking more broadly. I'm talking about living a life that is driven more strongly by curiosity than by fear.

One of the coolest examples of creative living that I've seen in recent years, for instance, came from my friend Susan, who took up figure skating when she was 40 years old. To be more precise, she actually already knew how to skate. She had competed in figure skating as a child, but she'd quit the sport during adolescence when it became clear she didn't have quite enough talent to be a champion.

For the next quarter of a century, Susan did not skate. Then she turned 40. She was restless. She felt drab and heavy. She asked herself when was the last time she'd felt truly light, joyous and -- yes -- creative in her own skin. To her shock, she realized that the last time she'd experienced such feelings had been as a teenager, back when she was still figure skating. She was appalled to discover that she had denied herself this life-affirming pursuit for so long, and she was curious to see if she still loved it.

So she followed her curiosity. She bought a pair of skates, found a rink, hired a coach. She ignored the voice within her that told her she was being self-indulgent and preposterous to do this crazy thing. She tamped down her feelings of extreme self-consciousness at being the only middle-aged woman on the ice, with all those tiny, feathery nine-year-old girls.

She just did it. Three mornings a week, Susan awoke before dawn and went skating. And she skated and skated and skated. And yes, she loved it, even more than ever, perhaps, because now, as an adult, she finally had the perspective to appreciate the value of her own joy. Skating made her feel alive and ageless. She stopped feeling like she was nothing more than a consumer, nothing more than the sum of her daily obligations and duties. She was making something of herself, making something with herself. It was a literal revolution, as she spun to life again on the ice.

Please note that my friend did not quit her job and move to Toronto to study 70 hours a week with an Olympic-level skating coach. And no, this story does not end with her winning any medals. In fact, this story does not end at all, because Susan is still figure skating -- simply because skating is still the best way for her to unfold a certain beauty and transcendence within her life. That's what I call creative living."

How are you living your life? Are you creating a life you enjoy or endure?

Like Susan, you may be doing well based on the world's standard but have lost the spark of joy in your life. You don't have to keep going in that direction. If you'll act now, and take control of your situation, you can reignite your life again.

UNLOCKING YOUR CREATIVITY ROADMAP

HOW TO FIND YOUR CREATIVITY

> *Growth is painful. Change is painful.*
> *But, nothing is as painful as staying*
> *stuck where you do not belong.*
> *- Narayana Murthy*

Pursuing creativity connects you to the moment, to your inner self, and to your Creator. It allows you to create something bigger than yourself. It gives you joy, connects your mind and soul, and brings out your best.

But how to find your creativity when your life is busy?

Creativity is like a muscle. It will grow if you exercise it and push it past it's limits. It is a skill that can be developed just like any other.

In the previous chapter, we talked about laying the foundation for your creativity. Now, it's time to stretch your creative muscles and find your creative idea. Although there is no one-size-fits all approach, there are proven ways you can discover your ideas and improve your creativity.

Here are seven things you can do to jumpstart your creativity and turn your ideas to reality:

1. Un-Busy Yourself for Ideas to Bubble Up

Ever wonder why some of your best ideas seem to come out of the blue, like when you're taking a walk or in the shower?

In the Fast Company interview about Creativity, Teresa Amabile said, "Time pressure stifles creativity because people can't deeply engage with the problem. Creativity requires an incubation period; people need time to soak in a problem and let the ideas bubble up."

Creative thinking does not arise from a busy life. When your mind is on the dozen other things you need to get done, you're locked out from that creative zone. You end up focusing on urgent matters or what needs to be done today, rather than on what you want to achieve in life.

Joydeep Bhattacharya, a psychologist at Goldsmiths, University of London finds through his research *predictive brain signals,* that the brain is most likely to gain insight with a steady rhythm of alpha waves emanating from the right hemisphere. These alpha waves are closely associated with relaxing activities such as walking, taking a warm shower, or even drinking alcohol.

For many of us, it's only during the relaxing time where we discover great ideas. Insights that's always been with us, but never heard because of other things we focused on.

This is a big challenge for me and many of us. Most of the time, our lives ar fully occupied with commitments. Routines control our days. If ideas come at the most unexpected times, we can't pay attention to them. When we're busy, those gaps of time get crushed out of our lives. When that happens, creative thinking falls out of view. To change this, we have to give creativity the time and attention it deserves.

2. Brain Dump Your Ideas

Before you can start creating your new project, you first need to figure out the details that you are going to create. This is where brain dump can help you to get started.

Brain dump is the process of getting all your thoughts out of your head onto paper. It is a proven approach that increases productivity and leads people to a much more creative outcome. As you write your thoughts down, you release some of the mental pressure.

To brain dump, you can use your electronic devices or the classic pen and paper. Choose whatever approach works best for you.

Write down every single thought that comes to your head. As you get those ideas out and written down, identify what makes sense for you and what doesn't. No filters. Just let it out.

If you are like me, who loves electronic versions of the paper, you can use the tools below to dump your ideas.

- Google Docs
- Evernote
- A Mindmap application like Xmind or Freemind

3. Practice Curiosity

Curiosity will lead you to creativity. Without curiosity, you will miss the ideas that pass right in front of you.

If you are just blindly going through life, even if you have the opportunity to thrive, everyday becomes a routine of sabotaging your creativity.

> *Never lose interest, never grow indifferent - lose your invaluable curiosity and you let yourself die.*
> *- Tove Jansson*

Look around you. Explore things you have never done before. Ask questions or collaborate with others. Be curious, and you'll be surprised how this simple act will give your creativity a boost.

4. Just Play

When was the last time you played like a child?

Being an adult and having more responsibilities doesn't mean we have to make life all about work. Helpguide's article described the benefits of play for adults as one of the most effective tools for keeping relationships fresh and exciting.

Playing together brings joy, vitality, and resilience to relationships. It can also heal resentments, disagreements, and hurts. Through regular play, we learn to trust one another and feel safe. Trust enables us to work together, open ourselves to intimacy, and try new things.

By making a conscious effort to incorporate more humor and play into your daily interactions, you can improve the quality of your love relationships—as well as your connections with co-workers, family members, and friends.

5. Play the opposite game.

"When looking for creative solutions, focus on doing things the opposite of how you would normally do them. Instead of seeing a situation as a burden, consider how you can look at it as an opportunity.

If there's something you dread, try to think—even if it seems impossible—about how you can bring some fun into the situation.
- Tiffany Moore, Life Coach

Playing the opposite game also means taking a different perspective. Challenge yourself by asking questions, like what you can do differently to shake things up.

6. Step Back and Reassess Your Life

Give yourself time to assess where you are, what's important to you, what you can live with and without. Most of the time, we keep going without really knowing what truly matters. Then, we end up heading for a big crash.

Give yourself a chance to breathe. Permit yourself to know who you are and what matters to you. Once you have the clarity, then you can move towards that direction.

In life, you get what you tolerate. If you badly want something, you will find ways to make it happen. Take the time to reassess your life and gain clarity, then you can work towards it. Will you choose to live a life by design or by default?

7. Create Your Mission Statement

If you want to boost your creativity, you need to be intentional. One of the best tools you can use to define what you want to accomplish is to have a mission statement. It is a roadmap for where you want to go and how you want to get there.

Stephen R. Covey, the author of <u>The 7 Habits of Highly Successful People</u>, suggested that we should create our personal mission statement. It can help define who you are as a person, and act as a representation of your purpose to other people when you are not present.

A meaningful personal mission statement isn't something you can just pull out of thin air. Here are some questions you can begin asking yourself every day that will move you closer to creating one:

1. *What is important?*

    What/whom do you value? How is your life connected to those things?
2. *Where do I want to go?*

    Your answer may involve a spiritual, mental, or physical destination. It might describe your career, relationships, purpose in life. Explore different areas in your life to answer this question.
3. *What does "the best" look like for me?*

    Describe your best possible result. You don't need to be realistic. This is your time to dream.
4. *How do I want to act? How do you want people to describe you?*

    Think of a few words you would want to come to mind when people think about you.
5. *What kind of legacy do I want to leave behind?*

We all have a legacy; the question is, how are you designing your legacy?

Imagine five, ten, a hundred years from now. What does the impact you've left look like?

If you need help in creating your mission statement, one of the great tools you can use is <u>Franklin Covey's Mission Statement Builder</u>. It can help you create your mission statement based on the information you enter.

These are practical ways in which you can discover your creativity, but remember there is no one-size fits all approach. Stay in tune with your mind and body. Assess when you are most creative and what ignites your imagination. Get the creative flow going.

ACTION CHALLENGE:

Now that you just learned how you can find creativity, you have to take action with what you've learned. Otherwise, you won't be breaking the pattern and be moving towards a creative life.

Write down your answers to these questions and revisit them often. As you continue thinking about them, start giving your personal mission statement a shot.

1. What is important for me?
2. Where do I want to go?
3. What does "the best" look like for me?
4. How do I want people to describe me?
5. What kind of legacy do I want to leave behind?

INSPIRATIONAL REFLECTIONS

If you haven't taken any time to create your personal mission statement, I highly encourage you to create one now. Here's a short story on how it transformed my life when I created mine:

STEPPING OUT OF MY COMFORT ZONE

A few years ago, the only mission statement I knew was at the company I worked for. I had goals set for the year based on that mission statement. I reviewed my performance together with my manager regularly. We assessed if I was on track or needed to make some adjustments.

In all the companies I worked for, one thing is common. Although employees support the companies' mission and vision, the process just becomes a routine check where the majority of the employees don't understand the purpose of it. Even if they do, many hate the process, and the majority are not engaged.

At that time, I realized I was thirsty for personal growth, and the best person I could rely on to quench that thirst was myself. My aspiration to develop life skills wherever I go, and something I would be proud of was always on my mind.

To fulfill my desire, I had to work towards it. And that plan all started a year ago when I decided to create my mission statement. After numerous revisions, here's the result:

> *Create and share materials that would inspire, encourage, and make a difference in the lives of people that are struggling*

> *in life. As I create, I allow myself to grow*
> *as an individual and a professional,*
> *have fun, build passive income, without*
> *compromising my priorities in life.*

I printed multiple copies, posted them on my vision board, office desk, and fridge. I kept it in my wallet and inserted it into the books I read to remind me every day of my mission.

I didn't have a clue when I started, but every time I saw my mission statement, I kept going. In those times I wanted to sit down and relax, enjoy watching or just let time go by, I chose to spend the time working on my goals. Even during those times that I felt I was at the lowest point of my life.

A year after I created my mission statement, things had dramatically changed in my life. I published three books, designed training materials, and built online courses. As I stepped out of my comfort zone, I saw myself growing, discovering my authenticity and embracing life to the fullest. My relationship with my Creator, myself, family, friends, colleagues and others got even better.

My perspective in life transformed. I learned how to make things happen no matter what circumstances I'm in. When I say that, I don't mean I will completely exhaust myself to accomplish everything. What I mean is, having the courage to be honest with myself. Knowing when to stop or rest if I need to, asking for help when I need support, crying when things are unbearable, shouting when I have to let it out, and creating what I want especially when everybody is telling me various reasons not to.

If you are serious about creating a more fulfilled life, you need to have your own personal mission statement. Many successful people, that created significant changes in the lives of others, like Tony Robbins, John Maxwell, Bill Gates, even Mother Theresa started with one.

Do you need some inspiration on how you can start yours now? Check out some personal mission statement samples below from <u>The 7 Habits of Highly Effective People by Stephen Covey</u>.

> *I will seek first to understand, for understanding is the key to finding value and value is the basis for respect, decisions and action. This should be my first act with my wife, my family, and my business.*

> *I want to help influence the future development of people and organizations. I want to teach my children and others to love and laugh, to learn and grow beyond their current bounds.*

> *I see each day as a clean slate, a fresh chance to write a new script and seize new opportunities. I value life's experiences and seek to learn and grow from each one. In my daily endeavors, I avoid neither risk nor responsibility, nor do I fear failure, only lost opportunity.*

> *I am a responsible spouse and parent; I give priority to these roles. I value differences and view them as strengths. I seek to build complementary win-win relationships with family, friends, and business associates. To keep these relationships healthy and to maintain a high level of trust, I make daily "deposits" in the "emotional bank accounts" of others.*

10
MAKING IDEAS HAPPEN

An idea can only become a reality
once it is broken down into
organized, actionable elements.
-Scott Belsky

As much I would like to say that inspiration and taking action to nurture creativity is enough, it is not. It's the starting point, but not sufficient to get you going. If you worked on a creative project a while ago, and you failed, then you lacked something.

What you need is a System in place. Everybody's commitment and discipline is unique. Many are committed, but still fail. The rest that succeed, what do they do? They have a system in place.

You don't need to figure it all out before starting. You don't need to have all the resources or wait for retirement to create what you want. All you need to get going is to start where you are and use what you have.

In the previous chapter, you learned how to find and explore the things you wanted to create. In this chapter, we'll focus on validating those ideas so you can take action to achieve them.

Here's your roadmap to make things happen.

1. Identify What You Want to Create

A good system serves a purpose. To build a good system, start with a clearly defined purpose. If you have done the previous exercise, you may have a better understanding now about what's the next thing you want to do. If not, I recommend you go back and identify one area you like to focus creating in.

If you're still having hard time despite the recommended activities in previous chapter, I encourage you to just pick one. Yes, just pick one. What's that one thing you want to create?

Don't worry about the other details yet. The key is to decide, take action and not get caught up in overanalyzing things.

2. Know Your Reasons

What you want to create should be backed-up by your 'Why'. Even it is something like *"I want to explore it"* or something bigger like *"I want to make a significant contribution in the lives of others,"* it is still essential to have that clarity.

By allowing yourself to understand why you will do what you want to do, will help you develop your awareness as you explore your creativity. Once you do it and you realize it isn't for you, then you can pick another idea.

The goal is to allow yourself to be immersed in the creativity process, until you find the one idea you will pursue.

Asking yourself several times about your why will help you have better clarity.

> ### *Know your WHY but don't*
> ### *get caught up in HOW.*

If you focus on how, you'll get caught up with the details and get overwhelmed to the point that you won't even consider starting.

In everything you do, I encourage you to put your heart into it. If your why is not aligned with your values, it won't motivate you to keep going through challenging times.

For example, money is one of our motivators. But most of the time, it is not sufficient to keep us going during difficult times. You need to have a deeper reason why you want to create. If your reason is money, why is more money important? What is the difference it will make?

Be specific, but you don't need to have all the reasons and answers. Many famous people, who made significant contributions to this world started out trying to make small changes. And that's what you're doing, starting small. As you develop the character and right habits, you'll grow into it.

It reminds me of the story of Mother Teresa. She wanted to start her work in Calcutta; she was asked what she must do to consider the work successful.

She replied, "I do not know what success will be, but if the Missionaries of Charity have brought joy to one unhappy home – made one innocent child from the street keep pure for Jesus – one dying person die in peace with God –don't you think it would be worthwhile offering everything for just that one?"

Like Mother Theresa, you don't need to have all the reasons why you want to create. But you need to have a clear purpose to get going. See <u>downloadable resources</u> for more examples and other materials you can use to identify your why.

3. Timeline

Set a specific timeline. Identify when you want to start, how often you will work on it, and when you will accomplish it. Once you define your timeline, break it in to smaller chunk.

Here's a detailed example you can use as a guideline:

Task: Work on my book project
Start: December 2019
Complete by: March 2020

Weekly Plan: Spend an hour for three days a week
Days: Tuesday, Thursday, Friday
Time: 8:00 pm – 9:00pm

If you plan it in a smaller chunk, like daily or weekly, you don't need to worry about accomplishing it based on your date of completion.

Add it in your Calendar, or schedule, and block it. If it's not scheduled, you'll never get it done. Making creativity a priority will activate the executive attention network in your brain and help you focus your attention on your creative projects—which is the first step towards becoming a more creative person.

Have a tracking plan. Keeping track of your progress will take time and effort at first, but the benefits of tracking are huge. It helps you stay focused on what's important to reaching your goal. It helps you identify potential obstacles and strategies for how to overcome them.

Once you've got into the routine and start seeing progress, it gets easier. Your progress becomes visible. Your confidence grows. You understand what you're doing is working and feel more motivated to keep going. People who track stay on track. Make sure you're one of them.

4. Support Group

Do you have trouble taking action in your life? Have you asked yourself why you haven't achieved your goals yet?

The truth is, you can't achieve your goals without the right resources and support. The bigger your goals, the more social support you will ultimately need to be successful.

Here are some ways to get the support group you need to achieve your goals:

4.1 *Get an accountability partner/s*

Accountability partners provide a powerful combination of support and motivation. He or she helps you to stay on track, gain clarity on what you want to accomplish, and verify the steps you need to achieve your goal.

Your accountability partner should be nonjudgmental. He/she understands relapse is part of the process, and you feel at peace with it.

Remember, your accountability partner isn't going to do the work for you. If you aren't ready to commit, and not willing to do the work, just don't bother with this process. Wait until when you are ready, as this will require a full commitment.

If you are dedicated to achieving your goal, plug into the power of getting an accountability partner. It's been an invaluable resource for me. I know it will be for you as well.

4.2 Join a community of like-minded people

Support groups bring together people who are going through or have gone through similar experiences. This common ground could be a community of people who are what you would like to become.

For example, join a community of authors/writers, business-owners, musicians, travelers, creative groups, performers, cooks, speakers, dancers, etc. We join a community to become more of ourselves by learning from and contributing to the community.

Being part of this group will provide you with an opportunity to learn from others who've been on a similar journey and to share your personal experiences and feelings. It will equip you with coping strategies or firsthand information when you encounter certain challenges in your creative journey.

5. Network with People that are Bigger Than You

Who are the people you are hanging out with? Do they inspire or motivate you to become the best version of you, or do they encourage to just go with the flow?

It has often been said, our network determines our net worth. Having a strong network or like-minded community is a principle of success.

You become who you hang out with. The people around you influence where you set that baseline standard for yourself. If you want to change your life, your network plays an important role.

It's hard to become what you don't see. If you want to be successful, surround yourself with success. Connect with people that are bigger than you.

Network with the people that inspire, motivate and challenge you.

Look for people who apply creativity in their lives. When you're around creative people, who live intentionally, the atmosphere is different. You feel energized, inspired, and motivated. The conversations you'll hear aren't the typical ones involving consuming, wishing, whining, gossiping, and mundane activities that take you away from achieving your dreams.

Good networks can expand your horizons, build your confidence, help you get fresh ideas, stimulate your creativity, and shorten your learning curve. They could advance your career, strengthen your business connections, and open countless opportunities.

Having a good network can be invaluable. It opens doors for you and allows you to enter into opportunities that are beneficial to your business.
-Richard Branson

If you're struggling with finding like-minded people, or want to expand your current network, you can use these tips below:

5.1 *Go to networking events, workshops, seminars*
A workshop or seminar is essentially a gathering of like-minded individuals who wish to achieve a common objec-

tive. Else, the individuals wouldn't invest time or money in the workshop.

Check the workshops out there, whether on the internet, online communities or newspapers. There are many hundreds of high quality self-help workshops out there – simply attending any one will allow you to meet other people who are passionate about personal development as well.

5.2 Use Social Media

No matter what field you work in, knowing how to network effectively can open doors for you. With email, LinkedIn, Instagram, Twitter, and offline events, you've got more tools and options for creating valuable connections today than ever before.

Know that successful relationships are built on mutual trust.

If you want people to work with you, they need to trust you first. You have to be able to truly offer something of value and expect nothing in return. Paul Teshima, co-founder of Nudge.ai, an AI-powered networking platform, said that "You have to invest in relationships and keep in mind that each person and each relationship is different."

5.3 Be creative in networking with others.

Networking is a two-way process, it requires "give and take". If one person does all the giving and the other does all the taking, it will be a short-lived relationship. Both parties must benefit the relationship to reach its full potential.

To do this, be creative in your approach. Each of us has something to offer. Start with what or who you know, do your research, find common ties or provide value. Show to the other party how you value their time by being intentional in your approach.

Remember, you only have limited time. If you want to accommodate the time to network with what matching your creative goal, you need to be very mindful of your time.

This does not mean you have to stop being friends with the people who have opposite views on life. The trick, hang out more with all those you want to become.

Prioritize and make time to network with the right people and choose what's best for your creative goals.

If you think you could be better at networking, then start small and simple. Try "nudging" at least one person a day, whether that's someone you've fallen out of touch with or someone you've meant to get in touch with.

5.4 Create, Execute and Repeat

Now, you have the fundamentals needed to make your ideas happen. It's now up to you to continuously build these habits and turn your ideas to reality.

Each step you'll take will help you get closer to fulfilling your goal. Following the system will help you develop the habits and character you need to make your ideas happen.

Remember, you can't reach big goals without big sustained effort. And when you fall behind, that's ok. You can't achieve the life of your dreams overnight.

Learn from it, get up and keep going. Create again!

INSPIRATIONAL REFLECTION

CREATE AN EXPERIENCE THAT BRINGS OUT THE BEST IN YOU

"What's the next thing I want to explore?" a thought I pondered for a while.

Once, while I enjoyed a warm relaxing bath, the answer finally came to me. I jumped onto my computer and searched for requirements to become a realtor. Ten minutes after my bath, I saw myself registered for the next exam and committed to complete six courses to become a realtor.

Since childhood, my mom taught me the value of real estate by becoming a landlord. House flipping, trading, or buying and selling, I wanted to do it all. I read many books about real estate investing and attended seminars.

My husband and I bought our first rental property years ago without using our own money. We watched the market and dealt with different realtors when we bought and sold our own homes.

I never thought of becoming a realtor, but I got so interested in the power of leveraging real estate investments. I worked with nice realtors, but I thought the best way to protect your investments was to know the ins and out of what you're investing in. So when that idea came to me, I took action right away. It just felt right.

Proud of myself for taking the first step, reality suddenly kicked in. I had to achieve an overall mark of 75 percent (minimum) to complete each course in the next 18 months. How would I find time to study? After I enrolled, my life commitments transformed. From having one child to two, working full-time, managing people overseas, not having my mom around, and more. I thought I could make it work if I dedicated time to study at night. It worked initially, but with raising a three-year-old and an infant, I was exhausted. That's when I recognized I had two options, either quit on my dream or find ways to make it work.

Determined to finish what I signed up for, I became creative and started leveraging my time. I didn't compromise my time with my family, but for other things like cleaning the house, I hired a cleaner. The time I spent watching movies at night became once or twice a month. I became more mindful of my time and learned the value of trading off entertainment for what truly matters to me.

I failed many times on a few courses, but I kept trying until I passed. A week before the deadline for my course completion, I passed my last exam. Then, I got my real estate license. But the story didn't end there; it was just the beginning. All the costs started to accumulate before I even made a deal. I interviewed brokerages and teams until I found the one that shared the same values and beliefs I had. I joined a team who would invest in my growth too. And in return, I knew I would have something great to offer, not just the split commissions.

In all my previous jobs in IT, I always had a flexible schedule. With the team I joined, I had to be in the office at 8:30 a.m. I found it extremely difficult initially with the age of my kids and nursing at night. I also didn't get paid when I went to the office.

As a realtor, you get paid with your deals and commissions. These were a few changes I had to face when I started, but as time went by, I adjusted my routine and my mentality. I realized I could come up with many reasons to demand what works for me, but if I wanted to from the team I signed up for, I needed to be willing to adapt to their ways. With a willingness to learn, I had to realign my actions to meet the desires of my heart.

In the first few weeks, I observed how the team worked. Everyone freely shared their thoughts about the real estate market, life, and anything. We had morning sharing sessions and affirmations, weekly book studies, and social gathering events.

I became a realtor during a seller's market. I witnessed multiple offers coming in. Being surrounded by well-respected and experienced realtors on my team, I saw different ways to negotiate and learned just by watching them. I also did door knocking, cold calling, open houses, stayed late at night when dealing with offers and many things that I've never done in IT.

I allowed myself to go through the process. At the same, I realized that even though I enjoyed learning about real estate, and gained valuable resources and networks, I wanted to focus more on investing rather than generating leads or buying and selling for others. I also missed the innovation aspect of IT.

I joined the team when I was on parental leave. One month left before coming back to work, I looked at the benefits, schedule, and the numbers I would make in my full-time job in IT. Although personal growth was amazing in my realtor journey, it was crystal clear to me that to make a living as a realtor wasn't the right fit for me. I couldn't sacrifice my weekends and nights and miss out on raising my little ones. Also, I wanted to focus more on investment properties.

When I realized that I couldn't do it full time, but wanted to stay connected with the team, I looked for opportunities I could innovate and give back to them. I offered ways to automate the training materials we had and shared the online-generating lead tools I used. It worked for both parties.

When I returned to my IT job, I saw things differently. I had a better perspective on life. I had developed life skills I neglected before, like making connections, taking on challenges, sales skills and most of all, I learned to appreciate what I have.

I may not have pursued that path of being a realtor, but I ended up getting another new development property from a person in my network. From now on, I know the people I can trust. I know how to negotiate for my investments. Even when I work with a realtor, I know the ins and outs of the business.

In the past, my husband and I felt we could have made more money if we negotiated well, but now, I am more confident with the investments we have. I also have the option to activate my license again in just one click if I want to, so whatever I did was not wasted.

I became more focused on reading books and applying them in my life because of the book study I experienced with my team. It eventually helped me to get into coaching and mentorship.

I gained access to valuable networks that helped me overcome the limiting belief I had, when it comes to what I can achieve in life and thus fast-tracked success.

That one action I took, when the idea of becoming a realtor came to me during my bath, led me to different places. The world of IT was so different from the world I explored in real estate. Because my world evolved on my job, I didn't realize the other areas of my life that I neglected. If you don't use it, you will lose it. This is true for the talents and skills given to us.

Allowing myself to go through these changes gave me the courage to pursue the other things I wanted. Like many of us, I have flaws. I shared my story because I believe that if you dare to create a change, embrace your imperfections, and go through it, it will surprise you how much growth you can accomplish.

By the time you reach your initial goal, many opportunities will be presented to you. The network you build and the growth you experience overtime will multiply a hundredfold. By allowing yourself to go through changes, you can create an experience that will give you tremendous growth.

So, the next time an idea comes to you, in the shower, or while having a bath, do something about it! You'll never know where it will lead you next.

ACTION CHALLENGE

What action will you take from what you've learned?
Remember, information is useful, but don't miss out on the essential part of the process — the execution. Go and take action.

Whatever You Focus On, Expands.

If you focus on the fact that you have limited resources, you will never succeed in creating what you want. You will be forever stuck in your dreamland. I don't want to break your heart, but the reality is the magic fairy won't come to make things happen for you. It's on you my friend, to take the first steps.

Start by making small changes, get better, connect with others, repeat the process every day.

Start your creative workout routine now!

CONCLUSION

*Life has no limitations, except
the ones you make.
Les Brown*

One of the big decisions we make every day is how we live our lives. No matter how you approach each day, either you live intentionally or unintentionally determines what you are creating.

When you stop creating what you are called to do, you end up feeling empty and unfulfilled. You will always be longing for something out there.

Why? Because you are here for a purpose. From the time you were born, up to today, you exist for a reason. Whatever that reason is, I truly believe that mediocrity is not part of it. I write this book because I believe that there is more in you.

You have a gift within that only you can give to the world. But you have to do your part to unleash it. Your ideas exist for a reason. It's a gift given to you, a partnership with your Creator, and other creative individuals to fulfill it.

As you come to the end of this book, I hope you are encouraged and also transformed. Remember, what you do with what you learn makes the difference, not only in your life but also with the people around you.

Step into your creativity and start regardless of the season of your life. Create now and allow yourself to set your gift free. If you want to create, focus on taking action, not the opposite of it – distraction.

Create an experience that will help you grow. Each of the people we have covered in this book faced different circumstances but ultimately progressed by taking constant action and creating a system that works for them. Remember, the secret of becoming the best version of yourself is to continue making improvements.

Today is all you have. Tomorrow is not guaranteed. Create a life that focuses on what truly matters. Live without regrets.

And last but not least, **let go of what's holding you back to create space for better things in your life.** You're not stuck. You can achieve whatever you want to accomplish. You can create whatever you wish existed but YOU have to make it happen. As Henry Ford said, "Whether you think you can or you can't, you're right."

If you haven't started creating what you want, now is the time. Let go and Create!

OTHER INSPIRATIONAL BOOKS

One Step At A Time
From Survivor to Thriver: Break the Cycle of Pain and Live to Your Full Potential...
Link:https://www.margediblasio.com/one-step-at-a-time

Get it now in Amazon

One Step At A Time: How To Turn Your Adversities into Opportunities to Achieve A Better Life turns ordinary people, who are struggling to survive each day into History Makers. People who make a difference, not only for themselves but also for the lives of others.

Take the first step to unlock your real potential to your best life!

TENACIOUS

It's time to Rise Up and Live To Your Full Potential!
Link: https://www.margediblasio.com/tenacious
Get it now in Amazon

In this short, quick read book, but full of inspirational and motivational words, TENACIOUS: Rise Up and Live To Your Full Potential will take you in the journey from darkness to light, finding your true self and living a life with no limitations.

NO MATTER WHAT IS GOING ON, NEVER GIVE UP... YOU ARE TENACIOUS!

LET GO AND CREATE

Want more encouragement
as you follow the Let Go and Create?

Visit margediblasio.com/LetGoandCreateNow

ABOUT THE AUTHOR

Marge is an author, coach, wife, mother, daughter, sister, friend, and a lifelong learner.

Known for her authenticity, genuineness, tech-savviness, and engaging presence, Marge specializes in leadership, technology, and creativity. She overcame adversity and many challenges in her life. Her journey became a guide to encourage others that there is hope at the end of the tunnel if you consistently take one step forward.

Marge is passionate about sharing her life experiences and bringing out the best in others. She was born in the Philippines, lived in Singapore for three years and is now a long-time resident in Ontario, Canada.

When not working or writing, she disconnects from all the technology and focuses on the moment. Most of her spare time is spent with her loving husband and two beautiful daughters, family and friends.

Connect with Marge!
https://www.margediblasio.com/

One More Thing...

Thanks again for reading my book. I would love to hear what you think.

Could you please take a moment to review it on Amazon or Goodreads?

Your feedback can help others to learn how they can benefit from this book. It would also help me understand how I can better serve you, as my dear reader.

If you know someone that could benefit from this book, do you mind sharing it?

You'll never know how you can save someone's life by simply sharing this book.

Many thanks,
Marge

ACKNOWLEDGMENTS

Writing a book could be challenging but very rewarding. This would not be possible without the support of others.

First and foremost, praises and thanks to my Creator, God, for His wisdom and guidance throughout my research and writing process to complete this book.

To my family.

My husband, Mike, who has been indispensable throughout the process. Thank you for being my spouse, friend, editor, fan and critic. Thank you for supporting me on late nights when I was writing. My lovely daughters, Arwen and Amelia, thank you for inspiring me to keep creating. Watching the two of you grow reminds me everyday about the importance of creativity. Having you both, provided me with a fuller and richer perspective on life. To my mother in law, Elsie: for your loving memory. You inspired me to appreciate the life I have and create whatever I want now. My mama, for your love, never ending support and encouragement for me. To my dad and brothers, especially Melvin, for believing in me no matter what I am working on.

To all my loving friends and community.

Thank you for supporting, listening and encouraging me.

Special thanks to Mae Flores, Marlon Mancego, Emily Sy, Jet Capinpin, Asmaa Dokma, Anita Oomen and other individuals who wished to be kept anonymous for sharing your stories. Your life story is an inspiration to others.

To the many teachers and mentors who have shared their wisdom through books, audios, videos and other online resources. As for the content and writing of the book, I have a long list of people to thank. Special thanks to John Maxwell and The John Maxwell Team, Marie Forleo, Lisa Nicholson, Jordan Raynor, James Clear, Jim Rohn who all have each influenced my thoughts on habits in meaningful ways. I encourage you to read their writing as well if you enjoyed reading my book.

To Let Go and Create Launch team for all the support and feedback you provided.

To you, dear reader, thanks for investing your time in my book.

I am sure there are people I have forgotten, but I keep an updated list of anyone who has influenced my thinking in meaningful ways at margediblasio.com/thanks.

NOTES

In this section, I have included the list of notes and references for each chapter of the book. However, things might change overtime and the references for this book may need to be updated. Incidentally, if I have made a mistake somewhere in this book, either in attributing an idea to the wrong person or not giving credit to someone where it is due, please email me at marge@margediblasio.com so I can fix the issue as soon as possible. Although this book has been edited and reviewed many times, I believe that there's always room for improvement.

CHAPTER 2: WHAT ARE YOU CREATING

1. Shelley Walsh, "How To Transform Your Problem-Solving And Creativity."SmashingMagazine.com, Jan 9, 2015, https://www.smashingmagazine.com/2015/01/transforming-problem-solving-creativity/
2. Linda Naiman. "Creativity at Work." https://www.creativityatwork.com/2014/02/17/what-is-creativity/
3. Courtney Carver, "Why It's Important to Be Creative." BeMoreWithLess.com, https://bemorewithless.com/create/
4. "IBM 2010 Global CEO Study: Creativity Selected as Most Crucial Factor for Future Success," https://www-03.ibm.com/press/us/en/pressrelease/31670.wss

5. Marie Forleo. Everything is Figureoutable. Chapter 3 – The Magic of Belief

CHAPTER 3 REDEFINING CREATIVITY

- John Maxwell. Intentional Living. Page 16
- James Clear, "Make More Art: The Health Benefits of Creativity," https://jamesclear.com/make-more-art
- *"Why Creativity Is More Important than Ever." ideou. com,* https://www.ideou.com/blogs/inspiration/why-creativity-is-more-important-than-ever
- Health Benefits of Creativity, https://relaxtheback.com/blogs/news/health-benefits-of-creativity
- Tori Rodriguez, "Creativity Predicts a Longer Life", ScientificAmerican.com, September 1, 2012, https://www.scientificamerican.com/article/open-mind-longer-life/
- Courtney Carver, "Why Creativity Is So Important", cheltdesignfestival.org, October 2 2019, https://cheltdesignfestival.org/why-creativity-is-so-important/
- Jocelyn de Kwant, "10 ways to find your creative flow and live a more mindful life", CalmMoment.com, January 16, 2018, https://www.calmmoment.com/mindfulness/how-to-find-your-creative-flow-and-live-a-more-mindful-life/

CHAPTER 4: FUEL YOUR TRANSFORMATION

- John Maxwell. Intentional Living. Page 18

CHAPTER 5 LET GO TO CREATE

- Raven Ishak, "6 Ways To Let Go Of Control & Enjoy Life More", Bustle.com, April 1, 2016, https://www.bustle.com/articles/147204-6-ways-to-let-go-of-control-enjoy-life-more
- Elizabeth Scott, "The Toxic Effects of Negative Self-Talk", VeryWellMind.com, February 25, 2020, https://www.verywellmind.com/negative-self-talk-and-how-it-affects-us-4161304

CHAPTER 6: BREAKING OUT OF SURVIVAL MODE

- Michael Michalko,"21 Ways to Kill Your Creativity", Creativitypost.com, February 11, 2012, https://www.creativitypost.com/article/21_ways_to_kill_your_creativity
- Thomas Oppong, "Start Doing These Things for Yourself to Transform Your Life in Less Than a Year", Mission.org, February 25, 2017, https://medium.com/the-mission/everything-you-should-start-doing-for-yourself-to-transform-your-life-in-less-than-a-year-7c4fc430358c
- Pawel Grabowski, "Analysis Paralysis: What It Is and How to Avoid It" UserVoice.com, December 22, 2015, https://community.uservoice.com/blog/analysis-paralysis-what-it-is-and-how-to-avoid-it/
- Ray Dalio, "The Difference Between Open-Minded and Closed-Minded People", FS.blog, https://fs.blog/2017/09/open-closed-minded/
- Kristi Hedges, "How To Keep An Open Mind", Forbes.com, December 17 2015, https://www.forbes.com/sites/work-in-progress/2015/12/17/how-to-keep-an-open-mind/#61e3b5a8418e

- Bill Murphy Jr., "14 Inspiring People Who Found Crazy Success Later in Life", www.inc.com,
- https://www.inc.com/bill-murphy-jr/14-inspiring-people-who-found-crazy-success-later-in-life.html
- Tommye Fitzpatrick, "Vera Wang Says Keep Your Feet on the Ground and Don't Get Ahead of Yourself", April 30, 2013, https://www.businessoffashion.com/articles/first-person/first-person-vera-wang

CHAPTER 8 – DEVELOP THE CREATIVITY WITHIN YOU

- Carol Dweck, Mindset: The New Psychology of Success (New York: Random House, 2006).
- How to Be More Self Aware: 8 Tips to Boost Self-Awareness" April 7, 2020, https://www.developgoodhabits.com/what-is-self-awareness/
- Kendra Cherry, "17 Ways to Develop Your Creativity." VeryWellMind.com. March 24, 2020, https://www.verywellmind.com/how-to-boost-your-creativity-2795046
- Angelina Zimmerman, "Shift to a Growth Mindset With These 8 Powerful Strategies" Inc.com, https://www.inc.com/angelina-zimmerman/the-8-tremendous-ways-for-developing-a-growth-mindset.html
- Saga Briggs, "25 Ways to Develop a Growth Mindset." OpenColleges.edu.au, February 10th, 2015, https://www.opencolleges.edu.au/informed/features/develop-a-growth-mindset/
- Carolyn Gregoire, "The 75-Year Study That Found The Secrets To A Fulfilling Life," Pathretreats.com, https://pathretreats.com/the-75-year-study-that-found-the-secrets-to-a-fulfilling-life/

- Leigh Coulson, "10 Choices That Lead to a Happy, Fulfilling Life", https://tinybuddha.com/blog/10-choices-lead-happy-fulfilling-life/
- Elizabeth Gilbert: Big Magic

CHAPTER 9: HOW TO FIND YOUR CREATIVITY

- Chenell, "How to Get Started With Brain Dumping in 2020", HustleToStartup.com, https://hustletostartup.com/brain-dumping/
- Harry Lorayne. Secrets of Mind Power: Your Absolute, Quintessential, All You Wanted to Know. Page 90-91
- Donald Latumahina, "4 Reasons Why Curiosity is Important and How to Develop It", lifehack.org, April 17, 2020, https://www.lifehack.org/articles/productivity/4-reasons-why-curiosity-is-important-and-how-to-develop-it.html
- "Create a Personal Mission Statement for the Life YOU Want", ProductivePhysician.com, July 10, 2019, https://productivephysician.com/personal-mission-statement/
- "How To Unleash Your Creative Thinking", challengesophie.com, March 1, 2017, https://www.challengesophie.com/blog/category/how-to-unleash-your-creative-thinking
- "The Benefits of Play for Adults", Helpguide.org, https://www.helpguide.org/articles/mental-health/benefits-of-play-for-adults.htm
- Ella Taylor, "13 simple habits to nurture your creativity", OllieMakes.com, August 23, 2018, http://www.molliemakes.com/home/13-habits-to-nurture-creativity/
- Margarita Tartakovsky, "8 Ways to Ignite Creativity You Might Not Consider," PsychCentral.com, https://

- psychcentral.com/blog/8-ways-to-ignite-creativity-you-might-not-consider/
- Deanna deBara, "How to be more creative: 6 proven ways to bring more spark to your work and life", 99designs.ca, https://99designs.ca/blog/creative-thinking/how-to-be-more-creative/

CHAPTER 10: MAKING IDEAS HAPPEN

- Francois Pretorius, "Networking–It Is a Two-Way Process," www.succeedgroup.co.za, https://www.succeedgroup.co.za/2017/06/23/networking-it-is-a-two-way-process/
- Alp Mimaroglu, "Your Network Is Your Net Worth: 5 Lessons on Building Stronger Networks," Entrepreneur.com, February 2, 2018, https://www.entrepreneur.com/article/303467
- Braveen Kumar, "How to Network in Today's World: Tips and Tactics for Creating Priceless Connections," March 30, 2017, https://www.shopify.ca/blog/how-to-network
- Liz Ryan. Reinvention Roadmap
- Neal Frankle, "What is an Accountability Partner and Why You Need One," WealthPilgrim.com, https://wealthpilgrim.com/what-is-an-accountability-partner-and-why-you-need-one/
- John Maxwell. Intentional Living
- John Maxwell. No Limits
- James Clear. Atomic Habits

www.ingramcontent.com/pod-product-compliance
Lightning Source LLC
Chambersburg PA
CBHW012207090526
44583CB00022BA/2939